"Every professional writer—and everybody who wants to be a professional writer—should have this book on his shelf."
—WARREN MURPHY

"Should be required reading for all writers from aspiring to famous."
—MARY HIGGINS CLARK

"I found this book surprisingly candid and very well-informed. I learned some things I hadn't known. It should be of help to any aspiring writer."
—KNOX BURGER, Literary Agent

"A superior book: clear, candid, down-to-earth, and writer-oriented to how the publishing process works. It will build both your insight and your sales."
—DWIGHT SWAIN, Professor Emeritus,
Professional Writing,
University of Oklahoma

FROM PRINTOUT TO PUBLISHED

A Guide to the Publishing Process

MICHAEL SEIDMAN

Carroll & Graf Publishers, Inc.
New York

The first edition of *From Printout to Publishing* was published by CompuPress, Inc.

First Carroll & Graf edition of second edition 1992

Carroll & Graf Publishers, Inc.
260 Fifth Avenue
New York, NY 10001

Library of Congress Cataloging-in-Publication Data

Seidman, Michael.
 From printout to published / by Michael Seidman.—2nd ed.
  p. cm.
 ISBN 0-88184-822-0 : $10.95
 1. Publishers and publishing. 2. Authors and publishers.
3. Authorship. I. Title.
Z278.S415 1992
070.5—dc20   92-9282
                      CIP

Manufactured in the United States of America

For my parents, Irving and Annie Seidman, who
saw to it that my process began;

For my daughters, Erica and Lauren, who show
promise of making it continue;

And for Elisa, who is the present.

Contents

CONTENTS ■■■

Acknowledgments

I have been fortunate to have been taught about publishing (and writing) by some of the best people in the business. I could not have come to this point without them and their lessons, and this is the first time I've had the opportunity to thank them.

Theodore Solotaroff gave me my first job on the editorial side of publishing, gave me responsibility, and then showed me how to use it.

Tom Doherty continued the education of the editor as a young man by encouraging me to stick my nose into every office in the company, and insisting that all my questions be answered.

Several writers must be acknowledged, because working with them taught me not only about my profession but also about my craft: Harlan Ellison, Otto Penzler, Donald E. Westlake, Lawrence Block, David Bradley, Thomas Chastain, Charles Durden, Dave Klein, Gregory Mcdonald, Jack Dann, and Warren Murphy come immediately (but not exclusively) to mind. Indeed, every writer I have had the privilege of editing has taught me something. Thanking them all here would result in a work akin to *Books in Print*.

All those writers who have shown faith in me, allowing me to publish their books and asking the questions which form the heart of this book, must be given their due here, and my thanks . . .

. . . Bill Brohaugh of *Writer's Digest,* Sylvia Burack of *The Writer*, Kathryn Fanning of *Byline*, and Ed Gorman and Bob Randisi of *Mystery Scene* have all encouraged the writings which form the outline of this book, forcing me always to something more. It is what a good editor is supposed to do for a writer;

. . . Ron Patrick and Ellen Purasson for holding my hand

as I tried to learn the differences between advertising, promotion, and publicity;

. . . Linda Quinton and Ralph Arnote for putting me in front of a buyer and letting me see, first hand, just what it is a sales representative faces everyday. (It isn't a pretty picture.);

. . . The members of the Dallas-Ft. Worth Writers Workshop, for their ongoing support of my efforts as both a writer and as an editor;

. . . The staff of the University of Oklahoma Short Course on Professional Writing, where I've had the honor of teaching and the pleasure of learning;

. . . Karen and Billy Palmer of Bogie's Restaurant in New York City for food, drink, a quiet corner in which to work, and their trust;

And, of course, Ted and Mary Lynn, and J. J. Lamb—the most important part of the process is keeping your own editor and publisher happy.

FROM
PRINTOUT
TO PUBLISHED

Introduction

■■■■■■■■■■■■■■■■■■■■■■■■■■■■■■■■■■■

A GUIDE
TO THE
PUBLISHING
PROCESS

Introduction to the Second Edition

In 1988, at a conference along the banks of the Boulder River in Montana, under a sky brown with the smoke from the fires roaring through Yellowstone, Rex Burns listened to me talk about publishing. He looked at a copy of the first edition of *From Printout to Published: A Guide to the Publishing Process* and, sotto voce, said, "You're learning. You've published your notes."

Whether the book or the lectures came first is moot; the fact is that getting this information into the hands of writers, both beginners and seasoned pros, is important to me. The more you know, the easier my job becomes; there's less to explain and more time can be devoted to things like editing.

Before I can edit, though, I have to acquire the book, and before I can acquire it, I have to negotiate for the rights. Because I do so much work with un-agented writers, and because some friends of mine were in the middle of a negotiation that was getting out of hand, I found myself more and more answering questions about points in the contract. So I made some notes for my friends and I looked at the notes and I thought of Rex. . . .

By definition, a second edition means that there are changes in the text of a book; otherwise it would simply be another printing. When it became sadly obvious that I would have to find a new publisher for this book, I tried to find something of value to add, to make it different.

The major changes in the industry are the shrinking marketplace and rising prices. Trying to reflect those differences, however, would be an endless process, so we've left the figures alone and the P & L balance sheet used as an example remains fixed in the old days.

Contracts aren't changing very quickly. Writers' organizations are trying to do something—clarification of certain points, better royalty splits, clearer royalty statements, changes in the reserve for returns clause—but movement is slow. And so, working with Kent Carroll of Carroll & Graf, we've added a new chapter on contract negotiation to this volume, based on an article that first appeared in *Writer's Digest*, which was based on the notes I made for a friend. I hope the information is as useful to you as it was to them. Keep in mind, the information is not legal advice; it's simply a guide to what you may find in a contract and what you may be able to do about it.

I would be remiss if I did not, at this point, once

again thank Ted and Mary Lynn of Sandia Publishing Company in Albuquerque for their faith and support when this project began and additionally thank Ed Gorman and Kent Carroll for making this edition possible. Very little happens in publishing (*any* part of the process) without the support of friends. I thank all of you, too, for being there.

—Michael Seidman
New York, New York
November 1991

Chapter 1

■■

THE
EDITOR'S
DESK

So it begins . . .

Never begin with a negative. Therefore, the postal service has neither mislaid nor mangled your manuscript and so, on this rainy Thursday morning, it has arrived in the offices of Bleak House, Publishers. We can all relax, now; it will take anywhere from three to six weeks before anyone looks at the package again. While we're waiting for the time to pass, let's consider some of the possibilities.

Many publishers refuse to read unsolicited manuscripts. Effectively, they are using agents as their first line of defense against the unpublishable book since it is assumed that agents read the manuscripts before they send them out. (I've had reason to question this assumption more than once. On the other hand, I've looked at some published books and wondered whether they had been read by anyone before release. We are nothing if not imperfect.)

Agented manuscripts *are* read first, before any others, with the exception of those already owned by the publisher; there are writers waiting to be paid for those, waiting for publication. As I said, we assume the agent has read the manuscript and chosen the particular editor because he or she knows that the book is somehow "right." Obviously, it isn't always.

If your novel has been solicited by an editor (and you've reminded him in your cover letter that he requested it), the manuscript will be placed in spot X in his office. (And perhaps this is the time to mention that I will be referring to the editor as "him." After all, I am a "him." In fact, though, at least fifty percent of the editors you may deal with are "her.")

The amount of time which will elapse between receipt, reading, and reply varies from house to house and from editor to editor. We try to get to these manuscripts quickly because, if it has been requested, we already have a relationship with you and do not want to put it into jeopardy. As you will see, however, the amount of work an editor faces each day—much of it, unfortunately, in the form of meetings which take up too much time relative to the results, even if they are important—means that a four week lag is not unusual.

The unsolicited manuscripts, affectionately known as slush, are, at the houses which accept them, piled in a corner and read . . . eventually. While discoveries are made—*Ordinary People* was found in Viking's slush pile and published—most of us do not expect to find gold within the dross. It is because of the low return for the amount of time spent that so many publishers refuse to look at unsolicited manuscripts. If one does arrive, it is almost immediately opened, placed in the SASE, and is back in your hands before you can say, "But you didn't even read it!"

When slush is read, it is most often by editorial assistants. They don't really have that much more time than the rest of us; the time simply costs less. Don't worry, though: Editorial assistants know what they're doing, are trained, and have editors looking over their shoulders. On those occasions when the slush piles are hip-deep and threatening to tumble, many houses hold slush parties. Entire editorial departments sit down around the edges of a room, the manuscripts in the middle of the floor, and everyone reaches in, pulls out an envelope and the reading begins.

In either event, perhaps one or two manuscripts out of a hundred are put aside for further reading, the rest returned with a form rejection letter. The form letter, bane of your existence, is a necessity. More often than not, manuscripts which are rejected are found to be unreadable. That is a subjective opinion, but much of the industry is based on subjective opinions; the objective criteria we can bring to our work—estimating sales, choosing a marketing approach, whatever—all stem from whether or not someone has decided whether or not you are a storyteller. But how do we tell you, politely, that we don't think you can write? The form letter, because it is an accepted business device, serves to inform you that the manuscript was looked at; protects the reader, because it is signed "The Editors," from nasty phone calls (we receive them regularly from disgruntled writers), and allows us to get the material back to you in a timely fashion—allowing you to send it to someone else, someone with the intelligence to recognize your talent.

So, your manuscript has arrived and survived the

screening process, has been given to an editor to read. It won't always be the editor you addressed it to, either. That editor may feel that another editor is more competent in a particular field. For instance, while I edit suspense novels, I have no feel (or sympathy) for the so-called "cozy." When I receive one, I usually ask another editor to read it. Then, if it is recommended, I will look at it from the point of view of publishing needs and consider it in terms not only of itself, but of the genre as a whole. (I might also pass it along to my assistant because I want her to learn and because I can't see the top of my desk. Come to think of it, I *can't* see the top of my desk.)

■ ■ ■

And so it goes . . .

The reading process, as I said, is subjective. After some twenty-five years in the industry, as an editor and as a writer, I still have no way of explaining why I like certain books as reading experiences. It is with just that kind of experience that your manuscript is first judged by an editor. (It has already been judged in terms of its appropriateness for the publishing list by the person who received it: I don't publish adult westerns, for instance, and if your covering letter tells me that's what I've got in my hands, I'll pass without looking further.)

When I began my publishing career, the editor I worked for told me, "Michael, there's a prurient interest which will drag you to the end of any manuscript you pick up. If you give in to it, you will never succeed." He was right. All of us begin by giving the writer every opportunity to prove himself, we keep turning the pages, one after another, reading and reading, and suddenly we discover that thirty new manuscripts have arrived and we haven't finished the first. Most of us then, those who have gotten over the initial fear of being wrong, those who have learned to trust themselves and their judgment, need only read a few pages before a very clear idea of what our decision will be begins to form.

I know within five pages and will, perhaps, give as many as twenty-five before deciding to finish or reject the book. That's said knowing full well that you've spent weeks or months in the writing and that you are undoubtedly screaming right now that we're unfair. So finish screaming, take a deep breath, and think about this:

Have you ever watched people buying books, especially paperbacks? I mean, really watched them? They pick something out of the racks, drawn by something— the cover art, perhaps, or the author's name, or recognizing a title. They read the copy on the front and back covers, they read the first paragraph or two, they riffle the pages to the end of the book, and then make their decision as to whether to buy the book or return it to its place on the shelf. That is how much time you have to capture your ultimate customer (and mine). As editors, each of us has to put ourselves in the place of that person staring at the racks looking for something to read. If you haven't grabbed me, I have to assume that you won't grab the reader, either. If I am wrong more often than I am right, I'm out of work. I'm not out of work.

Having decided to finish your manuscript, then, the editor begins to bring some of the objective aspects of the process into the equation. Not necessarily consciously, he thinks about the category into which the book falls, what his inventory needs are, what his publishing schedule is. He may begin visualizing a cover, he may think about other books to which he may compare yours, or other writers to whom he can turn for endorsemen,ts. He begins to think about what the publicity and promotion departments may be able to do for *this* novel, while having to deal with the fifteen or twenty or thirty or more other titles which the publishing house will release in the same month. He considers the competition, not only in terms of other books like yours, but in terms of what is going to be published at some future date—the date he projects for publishing yours.

The editor is thinking about the amount of work which may have to be done on your manuscript editorially, and how many other manuscripts he has pending which need work. He is thinking about how much he will have to pay for agreeing to publish your book (that's what we do, ultimately: We agree to publish your work. We do not really buy it; we lease it for a period of time), and what that will do to his budget. He is considering the conversation he will have with his boss or his editorial committee, a conversation during which he will have to defend his decision to acquire the rights to your book, to invest in something with no guarantees, even if you have a proven track record in the industry.

At some point the editor realizes that publishing—for almost everyone involved—is like sitting down to an all-night poker game and spending the entire evening drawing to inside straights. He begins to wonder about the wisdom of his career choice and about the availability of a street corner on which to sell hot dogs from a pretty cart. And then he shrugs, squares the pages of your manuscript, and marches into the boss's office, with the answers to all of those questions. (If he doesn't have the answers, he sits on the manuscript for a while. Usually nothing hatches, but it gives him time to think.)

While that part of the process is going on, your editor is also involved in dealing with the rest of his list—

working on the cover for one book, writing copy for another, talking to the marketing people about yet another. He is tracking the activity on books that have just shipped, is editing one title while checking page proofs on a second, is explaining to one author why there was no full page ad in *The New York Times Book Review* and to another why there were no reviews at all, anywhere, and yes, the book was sent out. He's dealing with one writer whose mother's cousin's daughter-in-law wasn't able to find the book in Los Angeles (but, no, no one has the name of the bookstore she didn't find the book in, and no, no one asked whether the daughter-in-law asked the manager if he had a copy in stock) and with another writer who wants his girlfriend on the cover. . . .

We understand that you are impatient to know what's going on, but you have to realize that any given manuscript is—from the publisher's point of view—a mote. Editors (generally) receive very little recompense for what usually is a fifteen-hour day, six days a week. I'm not complaining (well, yes I am. But I'm not about to make a career change at this point), I'm simply letting you know that those long delays are not personal nor is a rejection. It is the book that has been rejected, not *you,* and the long delays are the result of trying to do everything right. Just as Lincoln knew you couldn't fool all of the people all of the time, we know that you can't satisfy all of the people. Ever.

But we want to try. You can help, at every stage of the process. Feel free to call if you haven't heard anything after three months, but don't be surprised if the editor is "unavailable." Just knowing you called will usually get the wheels moving again. Send a polite letter . . . and hope that it won't take as long to get a response to that as it has to the submission. An editor has two things of special value in the eyes of the company which employs him: his editorial judgment and the authors with whom he works. The author/editor relationship is often a warm, loving one which will transcend the shifts which occur as both explore new possibilities in the industry. (A gentle way of saying one or another of them is no longer with the publisher.) Publishing has always been a buyer's market. It makes sense, then, to give the publishers and editors as much latitude as you can without losing your self-respect. If we can work together, we can get your printout published to everyone's satisfaction. And remember, too, that if you get angry enough, you have only to write or call and inform the editor that the manuscript has been withdrawn from submission.

■ ■ ■

"Honey, it's for you ..."

I started out by saying "never begin with a negative." There's no reason to end with one, either. That call that just came in, that envelope on which the publisher has put his own postage—that's the acceptance you've been waiting for.

Oh boy, are you in for it now!

Chapter 2

GETTING BOUGHT AND SELLING OUT

A game of give and take ...

I know, I know, we're not offering you enough. After all, didn't whoeveritwas just get a million dollars and her book wasn't as good as yours and, and, and. . . .

Dominick Abel is one of the ablest agents in the business. At a convention we were attending in Baltimore some time ago, I asked him what he tells his clients when they complain that they haven't received enough money. He smiled, shrugged, and said, "I tell them that every now and then God smiles."

It may not be a satisfactory answer for you, and it

certainly won't feed the family, but it is, finally, as accurate and sensible and right an answer as you will ever receive about the size of your advance. The advance money you are offered is based on the publishing company's best estimate of what your book will earn (with the editor being told to spend less if at all possible. Hey, this is a business), balanced against the cost of doing the book, the various expenses the company will incur, from overhead lighting to toilet tissue, from the editor's salary to the cost of an ad celebrating the publication of your novel.

And keep in mind, for good or ill, it is a buyer's market.

These are things the editor has been considering from the moment you hooked him with your opening paragraph, and he is going to have a pretty good idea of what the answers are before he puts himself on the line and asks for permission to bid for the rights. (At some houses, of course, the editor does not have to go to anyone for permission and is allowed to spend based on a fixed—and sometimes flexible—budget. Even then, he will have answered those questions before he spends the money. He might even be more demanding; he's drawing to that inside straight with what has to be seen as his own money!)

The editor's answers come from charts, computer forms, and marketing people. One chart will give me an idea of how much it will cost to produce a book of a given size. A form will tell me how many copies an earlier book by the same author sold. The people will tell me what they think they might be able to sell of a title, based on my description of it and its placement on my list—is the book a lead title or is it being released as a category mystery?—and what we are able to ascertain about other writers' sales, and what the market will be like nine months or a year down the road, when your manuscript is likely to be a published book.

By the time the editor gets in touch with you, then, you can be certain that the beginnings of a publishing plan have been set down. Those plans will change, but the editor is negotiating based on that program. As your relationship with the editor matures, as you become more comfortable with him (and he with you), you can begin to discuss that aspect of your career. You will also have some idea of what he—and you—are talking about. There are some wonderfully arcane terms in this industry—from buy-in to jobber, from die-cut and debossed to display allowance and real estate.

It is at this time that an agent is valuable for both you, as the writer, and for the editor. Indeed, for all that editors complain about agents and their demands, during the negotiation for rights we prefer speaking with your representative because we know that he or she knows what we're talking about and that there won't be arguments later. Usually. I recently negotiated to acquire a writer's backlist and, since the agent didn't mention it, I drew up contracts which gave me publication rights for term of copyright rather than a more usual five or seven years. The contracts were signed and then the agent discovered what had happened. Because of our relationship, and because I have no interest in hurting the author—and thus my relationship with him—we negotiated a rider to the contract. But I got something in return—a new book. You give a little, you get a little.

Unfortunately, many of the contracts drawn up between an author and editor directly end up being bones of serious contention between them in the future. We will take it for granted that you have some idea of what you are doing, knowing simultaneously that in all likelihood you don't. Therefore, an editor will perhaps retain movie and foreign rights for his company, rather than leaving them with you. You may lose something because of that. The editor's thought, however, is that you are not in a position to market those rights yourself and that your percentage, should the publisher place the rights, is one hundred percent more than you would have received otherwise. Agents, on the other hand, retain those rights (again, usually; there is nothing hard-and-fast about it, that's why it is called negotiation) and you will get eighty-five or ninety percent of the monies received, rather than fifty or seventy-five.

An agent also has a better idea of the fair market value of a manuscript than you do. The agent is in the marketplace on a day-to-day and even moment-to-moment basis, knows who is paying what for particular kinds of books, knows what an editor was willing to pay for a similar novel last week, and also knows what a publishing house is capable of doing for and with an author. It is often better to give up some dollars knowing that the "lost" money will be spent on the marketing side. The bottom line is that if the book is not placed into the market well, if it isn't where your potential reader can find it, you might just as well have left it in your drawer. Oh, sure, you've received your advance, but you won't be happy with the results. Then you'll want to go to another publisher, but you won't have sales figures to use to your advantage, and you are, for all intents and purposes, back at square one.

It is true that if a publisher spends a million dollars for the publication rights to a title, it is committed to spending heavily in the promotion of that book. We are not, however, talking about the seven-figure purchase or, for that matter, about the six-figure acquisition. We're talking about the difference between $2,000 and $5,000 or $5,000 and $10,000. At those levels, at the levels most authors are working, the commitment is effectively the same. This is the area in which a writer proves himself, sort of a Golden Gloves of publishing. The cream rises to the top. A book I published in

January 1988 (*Citadel Run,* by Paul Bishop) is an excellent example. A first novel, I paid in the $2,000 to $5,000 range for the rights. Because it was such a good book, however, I knew that I could use money not spent on the advance to give *Citadel Run* the kind of promotion it would not receive otherwise, and publish it as a hardcover rather than as a paperback original.

First novels have inherent problems on the marketing side, especially when it comes to convincing the bookstores to take them in sufficient quantities. It is difficult to get them reviewed. They are competing for space with proven authors. They cause great excitement when they work. By paying a little less, I was in a position to spend more than I might have otherwise in the promotion. As this is being written, I have every reason to believe we will be successful. In this instance, the acquisition was made directly from the author; happily, the author had been involved with the industry long enough to make some good decisions. (He retained movie rights.)

We'll be discussing promotion and publicity later in this book, but it is important for you to be aware of how every aspect of the publication of a book affects all of the others.

■ ■ ■

Getting ready to bid . . .

Having made the decision to acquire a book, the editor begins to do some paperwork—those charts, forms, and discussions we mentioned at the top of the chapter. (I know, a discussion is not paperwork, but the results of the discussion are committed to paper.)

First, we estimate the size of the book. For the example we're going to study, we'll figure 288 pages. That makes it more of a "novel" than a category book (a silly and mindboggling differentiation, I admit. But . . . never mind. We'll talk about it when we get to production.) At that size, the cover price will probably be $3.95. Today, in 1988. A year from now, it will undoubtedly be higher. And we are talking about a cost-out [the projection of costs for a book, before it's printed, used for budgeting purposes] on a paperback original.

Let's give the book a title: *The Lure*. It is an espionage novel, and the author has published before, so I can find out how he's been selling. See, any editor at any house, given a couple of hours, a good relationship with his marketing department, and the sense to ask, can get almost any sales information about just about any writer from virtually any publisher. One or two phone calls to the right people, a promise which will have to be delivered on later, and it is done. Based on what I've learned, then, I'm going to estimate a first printing of 100,000 copies.

Time for another rule of thumb or, given the fact that I have two hands, two rules of thumb: 75% of my first printing will be sold into the wholesale market; that is, to a distributor who will get my books displayed at the airports, drugstores, supermarkets, convenience stores—in other words, into what are still considered non-traditional book markets. The other 25% go to the direct trade: Chains like Walden, Dalton, and Crown; into local bookstores and specialty shops like New York City's The Mysterious Bookshop.

The second rule of thumb deals with the discount and return percentage for each of the distribution methods. (You didn't think you were going to get through a whole book about the publishing process without hearing about returns, did you?) These figures change, but today, based on industry averages, we can assign a 53% discount and a 60% return to the wholesale side, a 46% discount and 33% return to the direct trade.

What this means for us, right now, is that our wholesaler, buying the books at 53% off the cover price will distribute 75,000 copies of *The Lure* . . . and return 60% of the copies! (Actually, they only return the covers—it's called stripping.) Before you panic, these figures represent *averages;* it is certainly possible for books to beat the odds. If they didn't, we couldn't stay in business. However, we have to use the averages to make our estimates.

My cover art will cost $3,000. That includes the painting and hand-lettered typeface.

I will attempt to acquire the rights for $5,000 (half on signing, half on delivery and acceptance of revisions. In this instance we are presupposing that I have a completed manuscript.) I will offer a straight 8% royalty rate.

Those are my givens. Grab your calculator, then, and let's examine how all of this works out.

■ ■ ■

The numbers game . . .

The Lure

100,000 copies, 288 pages, $3.95
$5,000 advance @ 8%

Wholesale:	75M 60/53
Direct:	25M 33/46

PLANT

Editorial	$1,060
Art	3,000
Production	8,020
	$12,080

MANUFACTURING		$17,075
(Printing)		
(Binding)		

BREAKEVEN

Royalty Advance	$ 5,000	
Plant	12,080	
Manufacturing	17,075	
		$34,155
Divided by average net price of $1.93		$1.93
		= 17,697

PROFITABLILITY

Gross Sales	$192,563	
Estimated Returns	-101,140	
Net Sales:		$91,423
Manufacturing	$ 17,075	
Royalty or advance	14,773	
Plant	12,080	
Total Cost of Sale:		$43,928
GROSS PROFIT		$47,495
GROSS PROFIT PERCENTAGE		.5195
		or 51.95%

■ ■ ■

What they're all about Alfie . . .

While you're still gasping about that "outrageous" profit percentage, we'll go through the process. That'll put it in perspective, I think.

The plant costs represent preparing the book for manufacture. Editorial costs, in this case, are for proof-reading and copy editing. For my day-to-day purposes, proofing costs $7.00 an hour and we expect ten pages to be completed in that time. Copy editing costs $9.00 an hour, and we seem to average three pages an hour. Therefore, copy editing for *The Lure* will cost $864; proofing $196, for a total of $1,060.

We've already explained what the art costs are and, yes, they can often amount to more than the acquisition price of the book. (More on that later, too.) That cost does not include any of the bells and whistles: Foiling, embossing, step backs, die cuts. They would be manufacturing costs and, for this example, we're not using them; the cover will be simple and straightforward—a plain cover with good art. The extra steps can bring prices up though, often adding as much as $.25 to the cost of each copy of the book.

Production is the cost of setting the book in type, getting the cover ready to run, etc. There's a chart on my wall, breaking down these costs based on pages and print run. For this novel, it comes to $.0802 per copy, or $8,020. Add them all up, and that's the plant cost.

Manufacturing costs come from the same chart; this time it is $.1707 per copy—and that takes care of printing and binding.

The first part of the breakeven math is simple enough: Just add the monies being laid out up front, then divide by the average net price of the book. The average net price is arrived at by taking the wholesale distribution, multiplying it by the reciprocal of the discount, then multiplying by the retail cover price. Do the same thing for the retail distribution, add the results and divide by total units:

$$
\begin{array}{ll}
75,000 \times .47 \times \$3.95 = & \$139,238 \\
25,000 \times .54 \times \$3.95 = & \underline{+\ 53,325} \\
& \underline{\$192,563}\ \text{divided by} \\
& 100,000 \qquad\quad = \$1.93
\end{array}
$$

Looking back at the chart, then, you can see the breakeven comes at 17,697 copies. (All figures are rounded off for the sake of convenience.) Let's see if we're profitable:

The gross sales figure is the one we divided earlier to get the average net price. Estimated returns are arrived at by taking the print figure (again doing wholesale and retail separately), multiplying that number by the price, then by the return, then by the reciprocal of the discount, and adding the resulting figures:

$$75,000 \times \$3.95 \times .60 \times .47 = \quad \$83,543$$
$$25,000 \times \$3.95 \times .33 \times .54 = \quad \underline{+17,597}$$
$$\$101,140$$

Net sales, obviously, is subtraction.

Next, we find the cost of sale. The manufacturing and plant costs are known, but will the royalty be higher than the advance? (Lord, I hope so, because if I'm paying more than the book is earning, I'm going to *have* to get that hot dog stand.) So, we figure the royalty thus:

The print run, times the cover price, times the royalty percentage, times the reciprocal of the returns, then add:

$$75,000 \times \$3.95 \times .08 \times .40 = \quad \$9,480$$
$$25,000 \times \$3.95 \times .08 \times .67 = \quad \underline{+5,293}$$
$$14,773$$

The total cost of sale comes to $43,928. Subtract that from the net sales and we have a gross profit of $47,495. The profit divided by net sales gives us the percentage of .5195, or 51.95%. Did you notice what was missing in all that math? Did you notice, for instance, that no one in the company—not the sales force, not the boss, not even *I*—was being paid? Did you catch the fact that there is no promotion budget set out in those figures? No galleys to reviewers? (Galleys, by the way, can cost up to $15.00 per set.) No charge for photo copies of the manuscript because no author seems to pay attention to the clause asking for two copies? Right: There's no overhead at all. While it seems backward to do so, this particular formula for a profit and loss chart calls for the first 50% of profit to be assigned to overhead. A whopping one percent profit!

According to the royalty figure we arrived at, I could offer you, as the author of *The Lure,* as much as $14,000 for the rights. Doing so gives me no margin for error in the publication process: If our estimate is off, and we only get orders for a total of 75,000 copies, everything gets skewed. If we are more successful, well, we'll live with the skew, won't we?

It should also be mentioned here (and perhaps repeated later) that the 100,000 copy print figure would actually be closer to 125,000 (bringing production costs down minimally). The actual print run is never set until after the orders are in house, after the sales trips have been made and the accounts seen. We wouldn't want to print 100,000 and need only 60,000 . . . or 212,751, would we?

I'm going to digress here for a moment and discuss hardcover publication figures. I'm responsible for a dozen or so a year, and really don't do a complete cost breakdown for them. I bought them, in fact, to do as paperbacks, and want the hardbound edition for the added review possibilities, for the library sales (which is where most of the hard-covers I publish wind up. And I'm not alone in that), and because I can use the same type, cover art, etc., for both editions, thus amortizing my costs.

When I want to see what the finances are going to be, though, I guesstimate a price ($18.95), a net sale (4,500 copies) and a standard royalty (10%): The book will earn about $8,500, and I have that much more to play with in coming up with an advance. If I did a complete set of numbers, adding in and then figuring paperback shares in expenses, I'd be more accurate . . . and a certified public accountant. I became an editor because I hated numbers but loved words. Why is it, then, that I spend most of my day bent over a calculator?

If I were strictly a hardcover editor, however, I would have to do the same kind of P & L, try to estimate how much we will receive in subsidiary rights (the sale of the book to a paperback house, book clubs, etc.), and make it all "work," as working is defined by my employer. The numbers I've offered you, however, are sufficient to allow you to make an educated guess if you are conducting your own negotiations.

There is a third publication option: The trade paperback, a phrase which can refer to both a size format and/or the manner in which the book is distributed and accepted for return. The majority of trade paperbacks are paperbound hardcover books. They developed as reprints using existing plates and art and so were a way of getting expensive books into the hands of a wider reading public by bringing the price down. Some publishers have used (and continue to use) their trade paperback logo as a way of publishing books which they're afraid will not work in mass market or hardcover. Production is less expensive, the cover price is higher, and the expectations lie between the other formats. For most publishers, however, the trade paperback is an alternative to hardcover publication (some do a mass market edition later, though these are not as successful as we might want). The key to the success of the format lies in the fact that the books themselves, while strictly paperbacks, are sold in the same manner as hardbound titles. Not only are they discounted in the same way, but they are returned as full books, not stripped jackets. In that way, the publisher can use the returns for sale to the next customer.

Royalties for trade paperbacks are generally 7 1/2% to 5,000 copies and 8% thereafter. Cover prices can be as low as $3.95 or as high as the sky. Now, back to our deal, on which we're about ready to close.

Are you being cheated at $5,000? That is the kind of question which can make for some interesting conversation late at night, after too many drinks, with a group of editors, writers, and agents refusing to go to bed because we're having a good time attacking each other. In the short term, yes, you've lost out on $10,000. In the long run, however, you will be receiving that ten grand in earned royalties over a period of years and you will, of course, have sold another book or two in the interim. When Donald E. Westlake, author of the best novel about publishing I've ever read— *A Likely Story* (Penzler Books hardcover, Tor paperback)—and author of such criminous classics as the Parker series of hardboiled mysteries and the rather more soft-boiled Dortmunder series (*The Hot Rock*), first read the article in which I told the whole world about the figures we use, he called to thank me because no one had ever bothered to explain that part of the process to him (and for the life of me, I cannot imagine what we hope to gain by keeping them secret) and then to tell me that I reminded him of the character of Wimpy in the old "Popeye" cartoons. He was the character who said, "I'd be glad to pay you Thursday for a hamburger today." Don's feeling was that he wanted to get paid now.

From the publisher's point of view, the lower the initial investment, the safer the gamble. The surprise is not when a book does worse than our projections but when it succeeds beyond our fantasies. The reasons for a book's failure are legion and conjectural and have as much to do with our country's rising illiteracy rate as with anything else. (And the discussion of those reasons is another book.) I've spent quite a bit of time on the subject of money because, well, I'm a relatively quick study. When the most often asked question at writers conferences is "how much?" I assume that the query is foremost in everyone's mind. I also respond to the question by saying that it is the wrong question, that what you want to know is "why that much?" Two birds, one chapter section.

■ ■ ■

The rest of the contract . . .

Money isn't the only thing mentioned in the nine to twenty-five pages of a standard publishing contract. Royalties vary; we used 8% in our example, but it could have just as easily been 6% to 150,000 copies sold and 8% thereafter, or 8% and a jump to 10%, or 4 and 6 (which is the way it would be phrased on the phone). The split could come at 75,000 copies, 100,000 copies or 250,000 copies. Now that you have the basic formulae, you can work out the figures on your own; don't worry about the variances in production costs— unless we're going from 100,000 copies to 1,000,000 copies, they're not going to matter very much. They will matter (to me) if the print figure goes in the other direction. On a mass market title, 35,000 copies is the barely acceptable minimum order for an initial printing. Below that number, the publisher is losing money before the process even begins: He can't even cover overhead!

The next area of particular interest will be the subsidiary rights, which exist as much in the paperback market as they do in hardcover. Some houses, such as Tor, acquire books for both formats and make publishing decisions based on the staff's feelings of what would be best for book and author. Random House, on the other hand, would buy only hardcover rights, and then sell paperback rights to another house which specializes in mass market publication.

Up in the stratosphere, publishers often work together to acquire a writer. Recently, Elizabeth Peters—who was being published by Atheneum in hardcover and Tor in paperback, with Tor bidding in auction for the right— switched publishing houses. Just to make things interesting, Peters also publishes as Barbara Michaels. Atheneum was the hardcover (or trade) publisher and Berkley did the mass market editions. After a heated auction, the Barbara Michaels titles were acquired by Simon & Schuster for hardcover, with Berkley putting up a hefty sum in order to keep the paperback. There will be no auction; the books are being joint ventured, co-published, or some variation on that theme.

The Elizabeth Peters name and work went to Warner for both hard and soft-cover publication. While we (Tor) wanted to keep Peters, I could not come up with enough money on my own—both my hardcover and paperback estimates were too low. So, we tried to work with St. Martin's Press to do what Simon & Schuster and Berkley had done for the Michaels titles. We were outbid by Warner, which took all rights. The big loser was Atheneum, which has lost the subsidiary rights income. Peters was probably receiving 50% of what Atheneum received. Now she's got 100% of the money.

That percentage is one of the advantages to making a hard/soft deal with a publisher. Normally, you would receive half to three-quarters of the income received by your hardcover publisher, a percentage that holds when it comes time for royalty payments as well. With your hardcover and paperback coming from the same publisher, you may—again—receive a small overall advance, but you do not share the royalties.

As was mentioned earlier, if you have an agent, he will retain foreign and movie rights, placing them himself. (It doesn't have to be that way; I recently raised an offer by several thousands of dollars in exchange for the foreign rights for a period of eighteen months following publication of our edition of the book. If I don't make the sales, the author's agent reverts the rights and has the opportunity to sell them herself.) If you are unagented, it makes every bit of sense to let your publisher retain control of those rights. Who do you know in Japanese publishing? If at a later time you do sign with an author's representative, you can try to negotiate the return of some of those rights. If your publisher hasn't placed them, you will not have trouble, especially if everyone is interested in maintaining the relationship.

Audio/visual rights (most notably in terms of cassettes) are becoming a major negotiating point today and, again, I'd suggest giving them up if you are not in a position to place them: The old percentage of something vs. a one hundred percent of nothing argument.

There are things you will want in your contract, and, if they are not mentioned by the editor (who will take many things for granted), you should bring them up. You will want to see the copy edited manuscript and page proofs, and if you assure contractually that you will return them in timely fashion—usually two weeks—there should be no problem having it written into the contract. (Many have incorporated that into the boiler plate—the standard text—already.)

Few publishers will give an author approval of jacket art or copy. Guaranteed printings, guaranteed promotion budgets, and promises of tours are not part of a standard book contract. How can we guarantee a printing when the print isn't set until the orders are in? Overprinting is prohibitively expensive, both because of warehousing and because publishers have lost the tax deduction we were once able to take for overstock. Promoting a book on which there are only 50,000 copies in the outlets (for mass market) or 2,500 copies (for trade), is senseless—you can't sell what can't be found and at those levels, the books are not being seen by enough buyers to warrant promotion. Stephen King may be able to get guarantees like that, but most of us can neither make the demand nor meet it.

One clause calls for some attention: The option. Publishers want to know that they are going to have the first shot at your next book because they are looking at you as a long-term investment; whatever success is achieved is seen as the laying down of a foundation from which the next books will develop. There are several options from which to choose in the option clause: They all call for a first look and good faith negotiation. After that, we recognize that you might want to try your luck. Therefore, we'll request a matching option, which means you can't sell the book for less than we've offered and that we have the right to match any offer received. If you don't agree to that, we try for topping: We can buy the new book for some percentage more than anyone else has offered. If you don't agree to grant an option, it is possible that the offer will, understandably, be withdrawn. More than anything else, the option clause should be seen as a show of faith between both parties.

It is also possible that you will be offered a multi-book contract, a rarity for a first-time author. Under this contract, you agree to deliver two (or more) books to the publisher in a given period of time. There are a number of approaches to establishing the pay out. If you are being offered $10,000 for two books, for instance, you might be offered $5,000 on signing and $2,500 on delivery of each title (which amounts to the standard half on signing, half on delivery approach of most publishers.) The royalties can get tricky: Most publishers will, under multi-book contracts, ask for a basket—or pooled—accounting. What this means is that the two books work together toward earning the entire advance: You have to earn $10,000 before you receive additional monies.

You might prefer to have the books accounted separately, having to earn only $5,000 on each. It is the same $10,000, but if the first title works, you'll be receiving money earlier. On the other hand, if the first book fails, and the second works, you might find yourself in the position of making nothing more on the first. It may balance out; in any event, I have negotiated enough contracts both ways that it would appear neither has the advantage. For the publisher the advantage is in that earned monies remain in his account longer, earning interest. I've never known turning down pooling to kill a contract.

The rest of the terms you will come across in your contract are virtually industry standard: There are reduced royalties for premium sales, or any sale where the book is highly discounted, and for sales in certain foreign markets, where the rate of exchange necessitates it. There is a warranty clause—which is inviolate—in which you guarantee that you have the right to sell the book to the publisher, and that it contains no libelous or slanderous material. You will grant the publisher the right to publish the book for the entire term of copyright; however, check for a reversion clause, allowing you to take back the rights if the book has been out of print for a period of years. Generally, the publisher will have a six month grace period after the request for reversion is received.

After you've received the contract, certainly have a lawyer look at it, and hope that your attorney has some knowledge of publishing contracts. (I had a problem with one who kept defining "book" as a finished product rather than as a series of words typed on bond paper. Of course, in our original contract, the word book did not appear; we call it "the work." The change the lawyer made threw us into fits of hysterical laughter. Well, we weren't paying him $160.00 an hour.) Some new writers show their contracts to friends who have had books published. If you do, listen to what they say, but remember that their advice is based on what they've received for their books and your contract is for your book, an entirely different animal. Keep in mind, too, that the contract is a standard form, refined over the years by negotiations, by the influence brought to bear by writers organizations such as the Mystery Writers of America, Science Fiction Writers of America, and others, and is not designed to hold you in durance vile. While publishing may no longer be the gentleman's business people claim it once was, publishers are honorable. Usually.

■ ■ ■

An alternate universe for those who care ...

It is not a popular approach because it is Westlake's Wimpy comparison writ large, but there are publishers— and writers—who are experimenting with a royalties- only contract. A major mystery author sold an out- of-category book to his publisher for $10.00 against a straight 15% hardcover royalty. In fact, *From Printout to Published* is being written in the belief that I'll want a hamburger tomorrow and will be able to afford it because I will have an ongoing income from the sales. I don't know that I would do it again, I have to see what happens. And that is what the negotiation is all about, finally: Both of us are trying to cut our risks, lessen the gamble. How often do you think you'll fill that inside straight?

Chapter 3

THE
BLUE
PENCIL
BLUES

Words, words, words . . .

So far your editor has been a reader and a numbers cruncher (if those figures in chapter two hadn't worked, he would have played with them and played with them, trying to find a way). He has been talking to people about sales figures and looking at the angles. When will the editing begin? (The editor wants to know that, too.) What is the editorial process?

It is something which can fill a person with awe, in the old-fashioned Biblical sense of the word. There is no real training for it: Whatever you learn in an editing class is meaningless on the day a manuscript arrives on your desk, something someone has written—someone you are now responsible to—and something you are responsible for. This is not an exercise: People are depending on the outcome of your work.

The first manuscript I edited was by a former police officer, Edward Droge. Ed had been on the take and had been called as a witness before the Knapp Commission in New York City which was investigating corruption on the New York police force. His book had political implications as well as being the work of a sincere man who had done what he had done, felt there were reasons for it, and tried to explain them.

I lifted my blue pencil—and stopped. Who was I to change a word of this man's work? I could deal with the misspellings, the obvious grammatical errors (or were they style?), the errors of fact. But beyond that? I started with something easy, the title. Ed had wanted to call the book *10-14: Assist Patrolman*, based on the radio code for a call for help. I was told, and I listened, unfortunately, that the title was too obscure.

"Even with the subtitle, even with assist patrolman?" I asked.

"Yes." Period. The suggestion was to call it *The Cop*. I blanched. I knew Ed wouldn't like that; on the job "cop" is pejorative unless it is used by a fellow officer. We settled on *The Patrolman: A Cop's Story*. It wasn't perfect, it didn't have the punch of Ed's title, but it was acceptable.

Which left me at the beginning of the manuscript. It took me three months to work my way through the book, questioning every move I made, every deletion. I asked the executive editor of the company to hire a free-lancer to do the work. (We tried; she was repelled by the material and refused to do the job.) So I struggled and finished. The book was published and sold to an English publisher. I guess it all worked out.

Ed went back to college, wrote another book or two, and disappeared. I managed to forget until this moment that whenever we were together, there were two bodyguards with us, other officers protecting Droge because there had been serious death threats made against him. But it was part of the job.

The editorial process is awesome when you receive a manuscript from someone you've been reading for years, someone whose work you respect and admire, and are expected to do your job. By this time, though, you've learned that you know what you're doing, even if you can't explain exactly what *it* is, or what it is you are judging against other than the author's previous works. So you read, and ask questions and make changes. On occasion, as happened to me recently, you are told that the author doesn't like to hear that there are editorial problems. So you take a deep breath and tell the agent that you have to speak to the author and breathlessly you run through your list of questions and suggestions. And discover that you do know what you're talking about, because the author thanks you and makes all but one of the changes. That's part of the process.

Then comes the day when another famous author's manuscript arrives, and you discover just how incompetent he is. You realize that he has no idea of motivation (either in a novel or in life), that his writing is, at best, stultifying. But by now, we hope, you have come to terms with your position and you just do what has to be done. In the end, the author's name is on the book, not the editor's, although the editor feels possessive about the work. If the author is willing to face the music, the editor can make his suggestions, do his job, and go on to the next manuscript.

Ted Solotaroff told me something in another context during my days as his assistant on *New American Review*. I had been invited to read my poetry under the auspices of the Rococo Society of New York and I was then young enough to say yes. After saying that, I panicked. What was I thinking, standing at a lectern surrounded by "real" poets and reading from my work. Ted said, "Look at it this way, Michael. They are paying to hear you. By definition, then, you know more than they do." It worked then, it worked when I began to lecture at universities, and it works every time I become intimidated by the thought of putting pencil to someone else's paper. I'm doing it because I know what I'm doing.

The whole point of editing is to make the book as good as it can be. It is that simple and that complex. What is a good book? It is one which will not embarrass the author or the publisher; it is a book which will be read with pleasure by as many people as possible of as many diverse backgrounds as is reasonable. A good book—a good novel is entertainment. If there are going to be reviews, we want them to be positive. We want word of mouth, satisfied readers telling their friends to pick up a copy. (We don't want people sharing copies; that cuts into our royalties.) We want the reader to look for your next book.

There are hundreds, if not thousands, of horror stories told by writers about what editors have done to their books. (And editors have their horror stories, too. Oh boy, do we.) They are all true. There is no real, objective standard; there is only taste, judgment, and common sense.

You've written a book and rewritten it, worried about every word and phrase and punctuation mark. Your work has been read by friends and family (all of whom are encouraging you) and perhaps by the members of your writing group, by a teacher or an editor at a conference. Hey, this manuscript is perfect.

It may very well be. I'd be willing to bet, though, that some changes could be made which will help. I would bet that some changes will be made, no matter what. They will often be subtle, they are usually well-intentioned. But you can count on a suggestion or two.

■ ■ ■

Sharpening the pencil . . .

The editor begins "editing" with the first word of the manuscript. As he is reading, not only is he looking for that ephemeral something which gives him confidence in your writing ability, but he is making notes—often mental—about things which trouble him, invisible seams in the story line, dialogue out of character, and conventions misused in genre fiction. These reactions become the first part of the shared editorial process.

If the book you've just sold to the publisher is a first novel, the odds are strongly in favor of the sale having been made based on a completed manuscript. Most acquiring editors are hesitant to commit to an unknown on the basis of synopsis and chapters; we can tell you have the idea, but we really don't know if you can finish the book. So, while legend has it that Robert Ludlum can receive a million dollars for writing three words in the center of a page, the rest of us have to prove ourselves. That being the situation, a good editor will have discussed his early reactions with you before making an offer for the rights.

This might loosely be called the concept editing stage. We're not worried about the finer points yet, about anachronisms which may have crept into the story line, about characters' names changing. These are broad strokes on the canvas, the movement of scenes because your closing is more suitable as a hook to open the action, or changing settings, or adding or amending character traits because it will make the story stronger.

A certain amount of this is fine; but pay close attention. Is the editor asking for something you haven't written? Is the story changing from historical fiction to contemporary romance? Do you want to make those changes? If you've gone ahead with the negotiation and sold the book, obviously you agree with the editor's concept. I mention this so that you don't turn around later and turn it into a horror story. I mention it, too, because it points out one of the advantages of the synopsis and outline approach to writing.

Once, not too long ago, I was working free lance for one of the paperback publishers. A writer I had worked with before, one I knew could get successfully from the beginning to the end of a story, submitted an outline which I rejected, pointing out that there were some serious plot flaws—some obvious, others of the kind where an editorial sixth sense indicated that things would go wrong—and that I just didn't think this novel would work. Because I was not there full time, however, and because another editor had given him a go-ahead, the author finished the novel based on his original concept.

Move ahead in time. I'm now employed by the publisher in question and one of the first projects to land on my desk is the novel, now completed. And flawed: the wrong character was killed in the first chapter. There was no way of salvaging the novel without rewriting it from start to finish, making it a different book—something I would never do because it runs counter to my beliefs about the editor's function. I rejected it, mentioning the problems, just in case he wanted to take it upon himself to begin anew. It languishes still in the author's desk drawer.

If the author had listened to my advice in the beginning, you would have found the novel on the racks.

He would not have wasted three months on an unpublishable work. If the same book had been a first novel, submitted completed, I would have rejected it, with a request to see more of the writer's work in the future.

On the other hand, and there is another hand, exactly the opposite situation occurred during my acquisition of *Spree* by Max Allan Collins. Collins is an accomplished writer, with dozens of books to his credit. *Spree* was the first novel we would be working on together. Max sent an outline which gave me everything I wanted, and one thing I didn't need at all. The central character's girlfriend, a kidnap victim, was slated to die. We wouldn't know about her death for most of the story, but we'd have that loss at the end.

It bothered me. I had learned a lesson several years earlier when I published a novel by Newark sports writer Dave Klein, titled *Blindside*. There, too, the hero's love interest—in this case his wife—was one of the victims of a serial murderer. It worked within the context of the novel; it was important. It had to be. While writers admired what Klein had accomplished (the book is noted by Lucy Freeman as an example of what a psychological mystery should be), readers were angered by the bleakness of the ending. I still wouldn't change the end of *Blindside*.

But with Collins the situation was different. Nolan, the hero, did not need the impetus of his girlfriend's death, either within the story or within the series in which he will be featured. I suggested to Max that she survive.

The author carped. The author disagreed. I told him to go ahead and write and that when it came time to write the scene, he should stop and consider the options. She survived. The author thanked me. I had fulfilled my role.

■ ■ ■

The editor's function . . .

There are editors who feel it is their job to make a change in almost every line you've typed. I often get the sense that what they are doing is forcing you to write the book they, themselves, want to write. Other editors, the ones I think you want to work with, want you to write your story to the best of your ability. It looks awful in black-and-white (though it seems to sound good when I say it at conferences), but the ideal situation is one in which the editor recognizes that you, as the writer, are playing God, creating universes, peopling them, and then controlling the fates of your creations. The editor's job, in that situation, is to be one of the angels assisting in the creation. He must be selfless, understanding, concerned, and remember that he is working for you as much as he is for the company which employs him. Decisions should not be capricious, even if they can't be explained beyond saying, "This just doesn't feel right." And they must never be dictatorial. (I hope my editors are reading this chapter carefully.)

The concept editing stage is often the most difficult because every change may necessitate another. Adding a scene to show one character's influence on another results in having to take out a later exchange, or adding still another. Giving a character a stronger role in the story may mean adding to every scene in which that character appears. It is the kind of work you will be asked to do; most editors would not take it upon themselves to create scenes in context. (Although it does happen, depending on the relationship with the author and the editor's own ability to capture the author's style. It is a rare and special occurrence.)

If you don't understand why something is being requested, ask. It is, after all, your book. If you are uncomfortable with the answers, if you don't like what is being done to the novel, you probably shouldn't sell it to that editor. (If you receive the same comments from all the publishers you submit to, however, it might be worth your while to pay a little bit of attention.)

Concept editing can be a lot of fun for everyone involved. It is an extremely creative time, with a fast flowing exchange of ideas, each comment and suggestion leading to something else. And it doesn't necessarily mean that there will be wholesale slaughter on your pages. Usually, if the editor feels that there is too much work to be done, or if the work will destroy the author's intent, he will not acquire the book.

Several years ago the late Stanley Ellin, one of the finest suspense writers this country ever produced, wrote a novel titled *The Dark Fantastic.* It was turned down by every publisher he showed it to because the theme was racism, the central character sympathetic, and editors were, frankly, frightened. Having Ellin rewrite the book to remove the sociological onus would have been to destroy the novel. The story was the man and his reactions and there was no way around it. As will happen with any worthwhile book, however, it eventually found a publisher who did not confuse the writer with the character and who had faith in the ability of the reading public to do the same thing. Common sense and judgment, again.

Most editing is done at home (editors have to do something between 8:00 PM and midnight, don't we?), and while one part of us cries out to work closely with authors, another part recognizes that we can only do so much. We pick and choose carefully so that the writers we do work with are the ones we believe to have the most promise—as friends, as associates, and as moneymakers. With that in mind, you can begin to understand why we hesitate to acquire properties which will give us more work with nothing to show for it.

■ ■ ■

But a Police .38 doesn't have a safety . . .

The next step is generally called the line edit. Now the editor is reading every word, listening to the rhythms of each sentence, and using his particular expertise to catch errors. It is less intense than copy editing (most editors don't spend too much time worrying about spelling and grammar), but it is a careful scrutiny of what you've written. Sometimes we catch obvious mistakes of fact (driving east when we should be driving west), sometimes less obvious ones.

In a novel I was reading for reprint consideration, the author has a young man, a police cadet, setting the safety on his revolver and then putting it down the front of his pants. Because of my background, I knew the Police .38 didn't have a safety; I also knew that anyone who had handled a firearm more than once would think twice—maybe three times—before shoving it down into his groin. It was too late in this instance; the book was released in hardcover long before I read it. If it had been an original title, however, and I had been the editor, I would have caught that and would have had the weapon changed (to perhaps an automatic with the clip removed) and found somewhere else to carry it.

Most editors have areas of expertise. Science fiction editors, especially, were fans, first. They know most, if not all, of the sources, the background, the roots of the genre. Other editors, realizing that they are working more and more within a category, go out and learn everything they can about mysteries, westerns, romance. Whatever the area, there are people to turn to for the information you lack. The more you learn, the better able you are to serve your writers. That is the knowledge you bring to the line edit.

The changes the editor is making now may consist of removing a word or two, perhaps removing a paragraph or passage because it is slowing down the action without contributing anything to the impact of the novel, adding a word because it helps explain what might otherwise be an obscure reference. None of these changes make a difference in your storytelling, just in the way the story is told. Sometimes we discuss these changes with writers beforehand; more often, you discover them when you are reading the copy edited manuscript. Again, you have the right to ask why something was done, but try not to be picayune: Don't argue against a change because it is a change. Discuss them and save your arguments for those times when the editing has hurt the book as you see it. And be ready to explain why; your editor can explain why they don't.

The first two stages of the editorial process deal with the book as a whole, with the story, with readability. They are part of a creative experience. Then comes copy editing.

■ ■ ■

Dotting the "t's" and crossing the "i's"

Editors and authors have one special common bond: We all have problems with copy editors. It may not be fair, but we hand the edited manuscript over for the next part of the process filled with fear . . . and often loathing.

What a copy editor is supposed to do is check spelling, check grammar, check facts. Your editor may not have caught your error in saying that a character drove from Chicago to New York in four hours; your copy editor has to. When you are dealing with historical characters, the copy editor makes certain you have them in the right time and place. The copy editor is a

walking Style Book, coupled with a dictionary, alma-
nac, and encyclopedia. After checking the facts, after
making corrections based on fact, the job is supposed
to be done. Anything else is supposed to be queried.
If the job is done correctly, you will receive the copy
edited manuscript from your editor, and discover blue
or pink or yellow flags stuck to the pages, each flag
with a question for you to answer.

You begin reading, filled with excitement. Here's
proof that your book is real, that it is actually going to
happen. And there, on page two, the dialogue has been
changed, "ain't" is changed to "isn't"; on page four,
the character is drinking tea, not bourbon; on page
five . . . It doesn't matter what is happening on page
five, you have no idea at all of what is going on with
your book. Neither does your editor.

For reasons obscured by the mists of time, many
copy editors feel it is part of their job to edit, to change
things they don't like, regardless of the facts. We try
to prevent it; I will often attach a note to a manuscript
indicating that no changes should be made in dialogue,
for instance, where this problem seems to crop up most
often. I don't know why copy editors feel that everyone
is supposed to speak the King's English (or is it the
Queen's?), or why they seem to assume that no one
has read the manuscript before they received it. But
they do. Sometimes, the results can be horrendous.

Bon Marché by Chet Hagan, is the first volume in a
saga about America, told through the experiences of a
young French deserter who comes here to witness the
surrender of Cornwallis at Yorktown and stays to
found a dynasty. The first thing the copy editor did
was change the name of the ship Dupree sailed on
because, as far as she could ascertain, the name of the
ship was not a "real" word in French. It may not have
been a real word, but it was a real ship.

Then, because she felt that "women readers will not

be sympathetic to some of the characters' comments," she changed them. The fact that in the 1700s men did not pay particular attention to feminist ideals seemed to have escaped her. But throughout the 800 pages of the manuscript, she changed his words and attitudes.

It goes without saying that she changed his feelings about slavery, too.

She did not like the author's approach to writing about horse breeding, even though he is a breeder. Changed.

She did not like one of the women. Changed.

When the author quoted from historical documents and period letters, she changed spellings, words, and structure, even though it was obvious that the material existed in the form that it was quoted.

When, in a love scene, one of the characters recited a Shakespeare sonnet, she removed the lines because she felt that they slowed down the action.

When I sent the manuscript to the author, I thought he was going to have a coronary.

Usually, in a case like this, I would have "stetted" most of the corrections myself, before sending the manuscript to him for final checking and approval. I did some—the more obvious ones—and left the rest for Chet. We then had to spend two full days, working on a clean copy of the manuscript, marking the changes which were valid corrections and getting rid of the rest before we could send the book out for typesetting.

Because there were so many changes, however, the type had to be double and triple checked to make certain that the book was the way the author wanted it.

I no longer use that copy editor.

Someone else is. Maybe your publisher.

Not all the stories are horror stories, though. In a conversation with Elizabeth Peters, she spoke of a copy editor who has worked on all of her books; in fact, when Peters changes publishers (as she just did), she makes the hiring of that woman—on a free lance basis—part of the terms.

The copy editor draws floor plans of the houses the author is describing and then points out that, no, the heroine couldn't have walked through a door there, because it is a staircase. *That* is what a copy editor is supposed to do.

Obviously, copy editors are an important part of getting the job done right and, just as obviously, they are proud of the work they do. Most of the stories are like Hagan's, not like Peters'. That's just like your newspaper, isn't it? If it isn't scarifying, it isn't news. Your editor will try to keep the copy editor under control because he's proud of the job he's done.

And this part of the publishing process is just about finished.

•••

The power of stet ...

Once the copy editing is completed, the manuscript is returned to you. This is the last time you can make major changes, as well as approve or question the editing that has been done. You may have discovered that a character's name can't be used (because he lives down the block and is threatening to sue), or you have discovered that a building you used was torn down before the action in your novel, or you've suddenly decided you want the hero to kiss the girl at the end. Now's the time to do that, because once the manuscript has been set in type, author and editor alterations are very expensive—and you can be charged for them. (That's part of the standard contract, too.)

Many of the copy editor's queries will be valid, questions about timing or place or character shifts which you and the editor didn't notice. (They happen sometimes out of sloppiness and just as often because of a change on page seven which affects an action on page 307. Copy editors keep track of absolutely everything in ways that are awe inspiring, back-checking every word.) Answer the questions, either on the flag or by making a change on the manuscript page; your editor will give you instructions based on the publisher's preferred methods.

If something has been taken out which you want replaced, put three dots under each word to be reinstated and write "stet" in the left margin. I prefer being told about things like that when the manuscript is sent back to me; sometimes I'm the one who removed the material and I undoubtedly had a reason for it. Knowing that we do not see eye-to-eye on the matter allows me to discuss it with you.

When the manuscript gets back to the publisher, the production department takes over. At the same time, the rest of the company begins to gear up for what they will have to do. Naturally, much of the activity is taking place simultaneously. On any given day, the editor (and other people in the company) will be dealing with as many as thirty different books in various stages of completion. We still need to do some things to get your book ready for publication. I've been thinking about them all along; now is the time to start what may be the most important aspect: It's time for this little piggy to get to market.

Chapter 4

■■■■■■■■■■■■■■■■■■■■■■■■■■■■■■■■■■■■■

GETTING
READY
FOR MARKET

A watched pot is never published . . .

As many as six months or more may have elapsed by
now. You're getting impatient (is this ever going to be a
book?): I'm trying to figure out what to do with the
option book I just received and don't like. But you're
not concerned with my problems. Okay, we'll get on with
it.

Before anything more can be accomplished, your editor has to schedule your book: Give it a publication
date and a place on the list—lead, second lead, mid-
list (or category), or perhaps some kind of special or

"off-list" slot. The slotting dictates position in the catalogue (for hardcovers), order of presentation during the sell trip, amount of money made available for covers and other promotional possibilities, as well as indicating how many copies we're going to try to sell. The higher the slotting, the more commitment the publisher is making to the book, the more faith being shown. It is a key selling tool for the sales force.

Sometimes the slotting is virtually *de facto*. If the advance is very high, if the author is an established name, or if events force the issue (as might happen with a novel that is timely because of an election), the book might be a lead. At least. (This will all receive greater scrutiny when we discuss the sales conference and sales calls.)

At other times, books are placed on the list based on an editor's faith in the novel, and his willingness to fight for it. There are occasions when we want to give the author a shot, commit everything to "making" him and we will then go out on a limb, pointing out why a particular title can compete successfully against the new Michener or Francis or any other best seller we might be facing. (Sometimes we're smart and decide not to face them; it is a thin limb, believe me.)

Position isn't the only consideration, nor can it be dealt with in a vacuum. Generally, a publisher has between one and two years from date of acceptance of the manuscript to get the book into print and released. Once I know a book will be ready for production (if purchased from outline, it has been delivered; if purchased from a manuscript, all the revisions have been made), I look at my schedule as it exists, the books I have in inventory (owned, ready, but not yet in the schedule) and try to find a balance. Will *The Lure* make a month top-heavy with thrillers? Does the month offer enough books for a wide range of readers, men and women, adventure and historical . . . each house has different needs, a different demographic structure. At one house, science fiction and mystery may be considered mid-list, books put out with a fixed figure in mind (probably 50 to 65,000 copies or less). At Tor, and other category oriented houses, we have a separate publishing schedule for SF, another for horror, and a third for the so-called mainstream or general list (which in my case may be suspense, novels of the historical west, and anything else I care to throw into the pot).

It is not surprising, then, that publishing schedules are second cousins, once removed, to airline and train timetables, honored as often in the breach as in the keeping. We try to shift and alter publication dates before the books are sold into the market (distributors aren't very happy when we change our minds after they've placed their orders), but sometimes things go wrong. A cover might not look right when the proofs arrive in the office (or they may receive poor response from the sales force), a "better" book for the month is ready to go, or something else is happening in the industry which requires your publisher to rethink the plans for your book.

However, we do eventually create a working schedule, tentative as it may realistically be. With that accomplished, the rest of the company can begin to get into gear, outlining the approaches they are going to be taking in support of the books. One of the first things that has to be taken care of is the cover.

■ ■ ■

You can tell a book by its cover . . .

From the moment the editor began reading your manuscript, he's been thinking of it in terms of something else: Every other book out there, the competition's as well as other titles on the publisher's list.

There's a school of thought which holds that books are nothing more or less than boxes of, say, pain killer. Tylenol or Excedrin, Bayer or St. Joseph, Advil or Nuprin—two of one, a couple of the other and call me in the morning. Something makes us pick one or another of each set and we swear by our choice. We know that acetaminophen is acetaminophen, that aspirin is aspirin, but we prefer one and return to it again and again.

Publishers don't really have that advantage. There's little proven brand loyalty. Certainly, for mystery fans the logo of Mysterious Press indicates that a particular judgment has been used in the publication of the book, but a suspense reader will buy a crime novel from any publisher. Tor has a very good reputation in the fields of science fiction and fantasy, and is developing one in horror, but fans will buy the books published by Ace or Zebra with equal enthusiasm. What a publisher hopes for is a level of trust being arrived at between the customer and the logo, resulting in the reader perhaps buying an unknown author from "me" rather than "him." Still, if you ask someone who published the book they read last week, the odds are that they won't know.

How, then, are we to sell your book?

The first tool—especially in the mass market—is the book's cover. Think of the cover art as a billboard, calling attention to itself while surrounded by some four hundred other new signs every month. You may not be able to tell a book by its cover, but you had better believe that the cover is one of the most important selling tools your book will have.

The process varies from house to house, but the editor is generally the first one to voice an opinion about how your book should be packaged. At some smaller houses—again, Tor is a perfect example—the editors actually act as art directors, developing the cover concept, picking or suggesting an artist, and then riding herd on the painting until it is satisfactory. At other publishers the editor might suggest a scene from the book, or a graphic device (flames, a piece of jewelry) and then turn a copy of the manuscript over to the art department. Artists are then assigned and the editor may or may not have the opportunity to see anything until the work is completed.

The cover is more than the painting. Type faces play a role in the overall design, and color also has a function. At one time, it was believed that green covers did not sell. No one knew why; no one questioned it. No one did green covers. Now, people pretty much do what they want . . . but there are still fewer green covers, and I have yet to hear anyone in a meeting mention background color except when they want something specific. The conversations about the packaging for Lawrence Block's new novel, *Random Walk*, are, if you'll excuse the expression, illustrative.

Block's book is a "New Age" story, holistic, contemporary. It is about a man, and then men, and then large groups of people who begin walking across the country. They have no idea of where they are going. Or why. They're just walking and experiencing things along the way. When I read the manuscript, I knew immediately that I wanted a crystal on the cover and, held within it, the image of a striding man. (The first thing I had to do was suggest to Larry that he add a scene with a crystal. It wasn't necessary, but it wouldn't hurt. Happily, Larry agreed. I still haven't decided whether that should be considered part of the editorial process or not.)

We hold cover meetings once a month or so, but because of the autonomy we have, I was able to proceed before the regular meeting. What I proceeded to do was have a special meeting. What kind of crystal? Another editor, more attuned to some of the philosophies we were dealing with, suggested aquamarine, because it represents travel. Having the stone, and knowing the color, the background was chosen: A dark blue or violet would be perfect, allowing for contrast with the central image.

I contacted an artist, Manny Morales, whose work is distinctive, and with whom I had worked before. A few days after our first conversation he came to the office with photographs of aquamarine crystals and sketches of how he intended to use them. We chose the one we liked and sent him on his way.

Two weeks later he returned with the finished painting. The figure in the stone was too realistic, I felt, and there was a problem with the background. Rather than being solid, Manny had done what he is known for, blending and dripping colors together. It might have worked but for one thing: at the edge of the canvas he had used orange, and the shape made it appear as if the crystal were floating in front of a planet. The book looked too science fictional.

When he returned the next time, the orange had become several dark shades of blue. That was fine. But . . .

Because of the size of the central image, there was little room for type. At the top of the book I am going to have the title, below that the words "A Novel for the New Age." At the bottom, but in large type (because Block's name is one of my selling tools), Lawrence Block. The cover was going to be used on a hardcover edition and then blown down (that's what we call it. Whether we are talking about reducing art or type for a paperback edition, it is referred to as "blowing down") for the mass market publication a year later. The proportions were wrong.

That is one of the reasons so many books have solid color backgrounds. If we need more room, we can just extend the background. When we're dealing with a pattern, however, that becomes impossible. It took the concerted efforts of the entire editorial department and our publisher to solve the problem, curving the type slightly and placing the tag line around the crystal image. If we hadn't been able to work something out, I would have had to go back to the artist and have him paint out the pattern, and that would have been a shame, because it is attractive and eye-catching—and that's its purpose. (Since this manuscript was completed, the cover has changed again. Almost completely.)

Every cover has to catch the eye and also let the customer have some idea of what the book *is*. In the case of *Random Walk*, I think there is a market among science fiction fans, but a cover addressing them directly would have lost the rest of the potential audience, including the mystery fans who've been supporting Block's work for years. To a great degree, designing the cover is a balancing act.

What do you want to say about this novel? When you go to a bookstore and examine the displays you know subconsciously what kind of book you're looking at: Romances, horror, men's adventure; every category has a look and feel, advertises its presence and, if done correctly, shouts out to you from across a crowded room. (That many bookstores—especially the chains—keep their books by category, helps.)

The cover concept for the mainstream *Random Walk* suggested itself, and so do the ideas for most category fiction. We attempt to make it stand out, but there is little that can be done while remaining within the formula. How many ways are there of ripping a bodice? That's where some of the other tricks come into play.

Foil is the most obvious; indeed, many people are complaining that there are too many books using foil type and that we've defeated the purpose by putting it everywhere. The foils do catch the light, and thus your eye, but where they were once used to let you know that the book was somehow special—if we went to the expense of using foil, the book must be a lead—they are now thrown on in an attempt to save paintings that didn't work out. I guess it's a lot like using something to cover a poor complexion, to hide a blemish.

Another technique is the die-cut. This is still something special and comes into play when we want to show that we are committed to a book. And it is an expensive process: Usually, you have to get two paintings, one for the front cover, the other for the interior. Somewhere on the front a hole is die-cut, allowing the inside art to show through. While it can be beautiful and effective, there is a serious shortcoming, one which can eventually hurt sales. Die cuts are delicate. Every time the book is lifted from the rack, and then replaced, the edges of the cut begin to wear, then tear. Books with torn covers don't sell well.

Embossing adds dimension to the art, and can save a poor painting by making it pop. The most effective use of embossing I've encountered was on the cover of Stephen King's *Salem's Lot*. This was a blind emboss—the image of the girl's face was on the cover, but there was nothing painted. Again, we are talking about a procedure which adds substantially to the cost of the cover (for 100,000 copies we would have to add .0286 per copy to the production costs; embossed and foiled would add .0464 per copy); when the second edition of King's book was released, the embossing was gone and line art had replaced it. It didn't matter, the book had established itself, the investment in the first printing was earned back.

The various production options are discussed during the course of the cover meetings because some art ideas just seem to lend themselves to tarting up. The decision to go ahead is not always made at that time (we've still not presented the book to the sales forces and don't know that we'll have the support we're looking for), but it does give us something to think about when we're having trouble coming up with a cover.

That happens all too frequently. Espionage novels are difficult to package if you want them to look different yet recognizable and crime novels present the same problem: I don't like blood on my covers, and so avoid it whenever possible. On the other hand, I published an excellent novel about a murderer on the subways and, on the cover showed just an extended arm on the platform. I had indicated death without being graphic. It backfired: A major crime thriller (*Malloy's Subway* by R. Wright Campbell) was seen by the wholesalers as being simply a category mystery and my sales suffered in consequence. (It should also be noted that Campbell had just won the Edgar Allan Poe Award for best paperback original mystery, so the wholesalers were aware of him as a mystery writer.) As I said, cover design is a balancing act.

You are rarely invited to join us on the high wire. We may make mistakes, but we are also in constant touch with the people who are buying the books for distribution, and it is their feedback and reaction which guides us. Even if you and your friends don't like a particular look, if the wholesalers are taking it, we're going to accommodate them first. We study cover proofs regularly, seeing what other publishers are doing and have an idea of what we're going to have to compete with. If you don't like your cover, and are also unhappy with the sales, you can always blame the art director. We do. All the time.

■ ■ ■

Adjectives, buzz words, and hoopla . . .

Remember that guy we had looking at books on the rack, back when the editor was considering your manuscript? Before he began reading your words, it was the cover that caught his attention. That is why it is not inconceivable that the cover artist has received as much—if not more—than you. (Don't forget, though, that if the book does what we are counting on, you will receive royalties.)

Having snared our reader, there's something else that he looks at before he begins reading—the cover copy. On mass market titles, the copy is all those words on the front (and designers often complain that we've written too much and are ruining the art) and back covers and, sometimes the page one, or blurb page—the page of text preceding the title page of the book. (The word page appears four times in that sentence. Just thought I'd let you know that I'm aware of it.)

Hardcover books usually only have the title on the front panel, and the selling text appears on the front and back flaps and the back panel where we'll place previous praise, advance quotes, a good scene from the book or, lacking anything else, your photograph.

The reader has some idea of what the book is either because he recognizes the art or found it in a particular section or rack. The copy gives him specifics: Period and locale, style or genre, and some clue as to the action. (I expect that you know what I'm talking about; you *have* bought a book, haven't you?)

The copy is created either by your editor or by a copywriting department or free-lancer working, we hope, under his direction. The editor knows exactly who the market is, knows the readers he wants to reach and knows—or should—how other novels of the same kind are being packaged. Now, more than ever, your book is a product. A product is packaged. It used to bother me, hearing books referred to that way, but then I began using a word processor and know that the words aren't processed—like cheese food product—and accept the fact that a rose by any other name will still make me sneeze. The point is, don't worry about what it is being called; be thankful that it is being mentioned at all. Otherwise, you'd still be unpublished. There is an art to writing copy and editors speak of the rhythm of the words and the pacing—they refer to the copy in much the same way that you speak of your writing.

Copy also serves to make things clear when the art cannot do the job. There are times when the cover painting doesn't really say anything about the book, even if it is suitable. What does the crystal I described for *Random Walk* really tell you, especially if you are not marching to that particular drummer? Nothing. So my copy, which will appear on the panels and probably on the mass market edition as well, will say something like: "First there was *On The Road*. Then came *Stranger in a Strange Land* Now there is *Random Walk,* a Novel for the New Age," I've given the reader particular reference points: Both of the earlier books were—and still are—cult items. They were books which appealed to a certain mind-set, free spirits in a particular era. I have, I hope, created a desire in the mind of the customer to be part of something special, maybe a Publishing Event.

There'll be other copy as well, giving more details about the story, naming names, citing locations, whatever else I feel may be useful in piquing interest. As I sit here now, however, I cannot think of what those details are. It is just as likely that I cannot, at this point in the process, remember many of the details of your book, either. That's why, when I received the signed contract back from you or your agent, I created what Tor calls a title information, or TI, sheet. (I might even have written the copy at that point. Perhaps I should have. But since I don't know yet what the art will look like, or how much room I have—and because another manuscript just landed on my desk and is mewling for attention—I didn't.) The TI sheet contains a synopsis of the story, descriptions of characters, details which we will need for cover, for copy, and for some other very interested parties—the marketing department.

■ ■ ■

Someone has to make the editor look smart . . .

The terms will change from house to house, but you can consider the marketing department to be the sales managers (at least two, one for wholesale and one for direct), their staffs (and their rods, they comfort me), and the promotion, publicity, and advertising department(s). Callow editors always lump those three together, much to the chagrin of the specialists. Writers always want to know what they are going to be doing for them. We'll talk about that; and we'll get to know the sales people, too. But first, a word about what the promotion people are going to want from *you*.

When you've gone to contract, prepare a good biography. We like to know where you were born, especially if it is a small town rather than a big city. Where you live. The college you attended. Books you've published. This is information one or another of the departments will be able to use.

A good photograph is useful, if not always used, and reviews of previous books (if you have them) are a powerful tool for everyone. Do you have friends at a newspaper, or who own bookstores? Let us know. Let us know where you buy books. While you're gathering all of that material, we'll be thinking of other things for you to do.

Now is the time when we all begin working together. If the machine is operating properly, the editor looks like a genius; he picked this book, after all. If the machinery needs some oiling though . . .

Chapter 5
⋯⋯⋯⋯⋯⋯⋯⋯⋯⋯⋯⋯⋯⋯⋯⋯

BITCH,
BITCH,
BITCH

Waiting out the process . . .

This might be a good time to take a break; things are going to be hectic for a while, what with a sales conference coming up and all, so let's take a breath and step back a bit from the process itself for a moment.

If I were to tell you now that publishing is very much akin to throwing a pebble into a still pond, and watching the ripples, you might look at me askance. And you'd be right. It is more like throwing a handful of pebbles and having the ripples wiping up and over each other.

At any given time, all the processes we're discussing are happening simultaneously. There may be as many as a hundred titles in the pipeline, flowing toward completion, each at a different stage. An editor may be responsible for one, or five, or fifteen of them at once, and the editor is just about the only person in the house who consistently keeps each book in mind individually. It is the editor who always has a commitment to a title, in addition to a list.

Things change with the structure of each publishing house, some holding the editors at a greater distance from what is happening at each stage than others. But even in those houses which consider editors strictly as skilled crafts people rather than an integral part of the entire process, the editor makes a concerted effort to spread the word. One of the most exciting things for an editor and writer is when in-house enthusiasm begins to boil.

It can't happen to every book, or to every editor with every list. An editor's credibility must be maintained, every book is simply not the best to come down the pike. If we push too hard too often, we are not believed. Using moderation, however, an editor can bring each book to its own level. His relationship with everyone else within the company is crucial.

There's an old saying among military folk that it is when the troops stop bitching that the C.O. has to start worrying. Publishing has just gone from being a pond to being a battalion.

Editors know, as an article of faith, that the sales representatives are functional illiterates, unconcerned with the intrinsic qualities of books, those things which made us buy them. (We're wrong.) The reps, of course, have long accepted the fact that the editors are ivory tower nerds with no idea at all of what is happening in the country between the Hudson River and the Rocky Mountains. (Too often they are right.) The problem is that the editor has become proprietary about his books on the list, and wants them to sell. The sales department knows what is going on in the accounts, knows what is being accepted or not, and earns its keep by getting as many books out as possible, without creating returns.

The production department wants to know why the copy edited manuscript hasn't come back from the author yet; if it isn't here tomorrow, the book will miss the ship date. The editor wants to know why it took so long to get it copy edited in the first place, and why the copy editor did so much editing, slowing down the process.

The sundry promotion departments want to know when they'll have cover proofs and the other material they need to prepare brochures, ads, and the other support items. So does the editor.

Then you call. Your editor has the phone clutched between shoulder and ear, his left hand attempting to keep a stack of manuscripts from crashing off his desk. With his right hand, he is typing a tip sheet for the use of the sales force and everyone else with a need to know about the book. The boss's secretary is in the doorway to his office, telling the editor it is time for the conference rehearsal. And you begin to wonder about what is happening to you and your book. Rest assured: It is being taken care of, there is no stinting.

In the middle of it all, always, is the editor. In *A Likely Story,* Don Westlake's publishing novel, he describes the editor's role as being the only person in the company who cares enough to crawl across the publisher's rug, begging for something to be done. As your relationship with your editor deepens over the course of working on several books, you'll hear him complain about this, that, and the other thing, including rug burn. The complaints may be valid; so, too, most of the other complaints of all the other people.

Take them with a grain of salt. They are complaining because they care. They are complaining because, even if your book isn't important to someone as an individual title, it is important as part of a whole, as part of a commitment to the process.

Publishing is *considered* a glamour industry. That means no one makes a decent wage, we do it for the glory, the pleasure of seeing to it that worthwhile books are available everywhere in the country and that readers are aware that the books are there.

Publishing is *actually* a business, and the bottom line counts. More and more today, editors are being made business people. Most editors, though, realize that you are their business, their bottom line.

Remember: Without you, none of us would have anything to do. We remember it.

This has been a paid political announcement. Stay tuned for the second half of the regularly scheduled programming.

Chapter 6

....

WELCOME TO EAST RUTHERFORD, NEW JERSEY

One for the money . . .

Until now, your book has pretty much stayed in the house. Any talking up your editor has done has been to people he sees on a daily basis, the people who will be doing the work necessary to enable the sales representatives to call on their accounts and convince the buyer that his customers are going to want *this* title. In-house enthusiasm has been generated. As former Mets pitcher Tug McGraw used to say, "You gotta believe." Once you believe, you begin proselytizing.

You go to a sales conference and, there, tell it to the

sales representatives, the reps, the people on the front line, the people who, to a great degree, are just like you. You faced rejection every time you sent the manuscript out; the reps face it for you now. What we've got to do is give them a cover letter and an outline as effective as the one you used to sell your book to us. That's all.

Some publishers—and I think they are the lucky ones—have their own sales force, people employed by, and working solely for, the company. Maintaining a sales force, however, is an expensive proposition. You're talking about anywhere from fifty to a hundred people, their salaries and commissions, plus bonuses based on net sales performance. If a rep has too many returns in his or her area, he or she loses bonus money, and that's one of the reasons they try not to oversell, and recommend buy-ins based on the outlet's past performance. Of course, they have expenses (they spend close to three out of every four weeks on the road). They need a car. . . .

Other houses use commission reps. These are people who represent two or three or more publishers (the more they represent, the greater their income), attend the sales conferences of each in turn, and then go out on the road. Personally (please remember that, *personally*), I'm not comfortable with that distribution method. Of course, I'm not a salesman, either, but I don't see how it is possible to maintain a balance in the presentation of the titles of three competing companies. The better reps, I think, are those who work for publishers with diverse lists: A non-fiction house, a literary house, and a general publisher. Knowing their customers, a commission rep can sell the right book to the right bookstore without any conflict.

Finally, there are national distributors. These fall into two groups: Trade and wholesale. A trade distributor is a publishing house which uses its own sales force to sell the books of other companies. Most trade distributors are careful not to represent lines which will conflict with their own, and are as likely to represent mass market books as hardcover titles.

Most wholesale distributors began in the magazine business (which is still part of the definition of a wholesaler). Because much of the mass market appears in outlets they had been servicing, they began to represent paperback publishers as well. Wholesale distribution for hardcover books is virtually nil; as the P&L figures indicated, it easily accounts for 70% of the mass market gross sale (before returns).

Distributors, while charging a hefty fee (based on sales percentages) for their service, are a less expensive proposition for a publisher, and most of them do their job well. Editors would prefer to have a company sales force, because we'd have greater, and regular, access to the people. Unfortunately, we really only get to see the people working for our distribution company at the sales conference, and it's difficult to build a strong working relationship based on meetings that occur only two or three times a year. (Which explains why we have parties during the conference. And you thought it was because we enjoyed partying.)

Sales conferences are held on a regular basis, with *regular* being defined differently by each publisher. Three times a year, Tor meets with its trade distributor, St. Martin's Press, which is now our parent company, also (but that's another story altogether). Semi-annual meetings are held on a national level, with our wholesale distributor, Warner Publishing Services (WPS), with all the reps present and learning about the next six month's highlights. (Warner Publishing Services handles only books—no magazines—for a number of publishers, including Warner Books.) We have monthly meetings with the WPS executives.

Because mass market books are sold to wholesalers

on a monthly basis, the editors gather every two months and tape special presentations about upcoming lists, which are put on cassette and sent to each salesperson. That guarantees that the reps will have all the information they need about a book before they call on their accounts.

The month leading up to a sales conference gives a whole new meaning to the word Bedlam.

▪ ▪ ▪

... two for the show ...

In our more cynical moments, many editors are likely to refer to the sales conference as the dog-and-pony show. It is not that we don't recognize the value of these meetings; it is that they are, by any definition, a show. They have to be.

A sales force may, in a period of three or four days, be presented information about anywhere from 120 to 200 new titles. This will vary based on the number of lines being distributed, the size of the lists, and the frequency of the meetings. They are all different, even if many are in the same category. When the rep is selling the book, we don't want him thinking "a mystery is a mystery," even if it is. Each book has its own personality, just as each of the different writers does. Each book is special. How can they remember them, keep them apart? How can they present them effectively? How can we, the editors, make each title something separate from all the others we're going to talk about?

Back to the initial selling tool: The cover. Transparencies are prepared of each cover which will be presented. The only drawback there is the all too usual situation of a cover not being ready. It may be unfinished because the type hasn't been laid down; the sketch may have been rejected so the painting was not completed in time—the possibilities are endless and Murphy's Law prevails: If anything can go wrong . . .

In the days leading up to the conference, the production department, working almost intimately with the art directors, gets the paintings in, has the photographs taken and then, based on the schedule editorial has created, places the slides—right side up, please—in the projector trays. Holes are left for late pieces. And, if it is likely that the art will not arrive in time, stock art is chosen. The stock art is a file of paintings which have not been used, or which artists have supplied as samples, and we find something suitable, if not perfect, to flash on the screen. The last resort is a simple type slide with the title of the book and the name of the author. But it is not memorable, just black words against a colored background. Always, cover *art* sells.

While the slides are being made ready, the editors are busy typing up tip sheets. (I needn't remind you again that these terms are all variations on a theme. What I call something from habit may be called something else at another house.) The tip sheet is a collateral relative of the TI (title information) prepared when we went to contract. Title and author, of course, top the paper. Then there is a keynote, a line or two which the rep can use to not only remember the book, but use in selling. My "First there was *On The Road* . . ." copy is an example of a keynote, so, too, would be reviews, advance notices, anything to give everyone a focus on what is being discussed. If the book is a first novel, if there are no credentials, nothing extraordinary (in the simplest sense of the word), the keynote might be "In the tradition of _____" It is overused, it is boring, but if the editor has attained the proper level of respect and credibility with the rep (and through her, with the accounts), you can get away with it.

After the keynote, there is a description of the book, a synopsis, if you will, offering just enough detail to make the story appealing. Again, locales, periods, historical characters, anything which might catch a local fancy, is mentioned.

Then there'll be a section on marketing tips: Reviews and awards are prime movers, here, as are comparisons to other authors to help in easy placement of the title on the racks. If there are any special plans in the way of advertising, dump displays, point of purchase materials, or publicity possibilities, they are highlighted.

Finally, the author information that hasn't appeared yet; most important, where you live. The last thing an editor wants or needs in his life is an author who can't find her book in her home town.

These tip sheets, one for every title being presented, are gathered in a folder of some kind and distributed to the sales force immediately prior to the presentation. At recent conferences, we've been supplying partial tips: Only the title and author information is on them. The reasoning is simple: We want the reps to be listening to us, not reading. One of the things editors have to learn how to do is present a book in three or four different ways. We take one approach in the copy, a different one on the tip sheet, yet another in the catalogue or brochure, and a final one for oral presentation. I want the rep listening to me when I speak; he can read more about the book later.

While the editors are busy typing and finding new ways to describe books they've already talked to death, or, perhaps, refreshing themselves as to what the book is about (it may have been a year since he last read it, and in the intervening months he's read a hundred more to one extent or another), the promotion department is putting together its plans.

Working in conjunction with the sales managers and editors, the promotion people (whose primary function is to help with the sell-in, getting the book into the store) are preparing brochures, posters, and other POP (point-of-purchase) items, drawing up plans for dumps and counter packs, and designing schemes to make the retailer sit up and take notice. These efforts began some time ago, perhaps when the schedule was first presented, but they have to have everything ready for the sales meeting. The reps will be given, at least, samples of the items they will have as tools, and in the case of a dump, we'll give them a C-Print (a high-quality, usually four-color, print made from a transparency).

The production department is gathering cover proofs (for mass market, cover flats for trade books), placing them in publication order, and putting them in folders. These sample covers (flats may not have flap copy; paperback proofs have holes punched into them so that the covers cannot be returned for credit) are the first thing the customer is going to see, and we want the salespeople to be thoroughly familiar with them. (A supply will be sent to their homes; more about that anon.)

Simultaneously, each person scheduled to present at the conference is preparing his or her remarks: Editors thinking about what they'll say about the book, the sales honchos coming up with suggested figures, the promotion and publicity experts refining plans.

And the rest of the company business goes on, too. See what I mean about *Bedlam?*

⬛ ⬛ ⬛

... three to get ready ...

About a week before the conference, everyone gets together and begins to rehearse. Because of the number of books the sales force is going to have to deal with, the speakers don't want to say too much (it can't all be retained), they don't want to say anything confusing or unnecessary and, wherever possible, they don't want to present too many books consecutively. (Three is too many.) At Tor, where each of the editors is responsible for his or her own list, and the lists each have their own logo, there is a tendency to present all the science fiction, or all the horror, or all the mainstream, together. That is the way the books appear in the schedule, in the brochures, and the way they will be sold. So, we look over the lists, say, "I read that, I'll present it," and thereby give the listeners a break from the natural tedium of hearing one voice. It also helps prevent another common and understandable failing: While I can't say every book I'm doing is the best of its kind, I'm certainly not going to say that one is less than fine. In praising our line, we tend to fall back on stock phrases and adjectives. By splitting the presentation, other people's phrases get used and none get overused.

The books are, as mentioned, presented in order. Even though we know that anyone watching will realize that the first book is the lead, we emphasize the fact. "The lead for the month is . . ." It serves as a reminder that this is the book we're behind. Because of the sheer volume of information the sales force is expected to absorb, anything we can do to underscore the important titles is crucial.

After each title is presented, the publicity spokesman will discuss what plans, if any, have been made. Sometimes it is more effective for the editor to say something, sometimes it gets left to the marketing directors. I might say we have a beautiful display planned, then allow someone else to speak about it. We have managed to get the same thing said twice, reinforcing the message, without seeming to nag; again, it was the power of another voice.

The last speaker is the marketing director. She will

give past sales history—if there is any—mentioning that we sold 78% of the author's previous book, on a put out of 90,000 copies. Therefore, we want to get 150,000 copies out this time. (A sell-through which is that clean—a very low percentage of returns—often means that there were not enough copies in the marketplace.) The figures are noted, sometimes refined: Let's not ask for too many on this book, it isn't as good as the previous one. Or, yes, let's ask for more, we expect great review attention, the author is about to break out.

During the rehearsal we have the chance to listen to ourselves, to get the rough spots out of the presentations. We might discover a good line—there is a lot of banter during the run through because we are beginning to get nervous and take refuge in bad jokes, some of which work—or realize that we're repeating ourselves, saying the same things about certain titles. We try to foresee—hopeless task—the questions the reps might ask. We'll look at a slide and decide the cover doesn't work after all and that we should emboss it.

We may try to find out what the competition will be publishing at the same time, either to ride their coattails or to prevent them from riding ours. We run the whole bloody thing up the flagpole and see if anybody notices. Because if they don't . . .

■ ■ ■

. . . and four to go . . .

Finally, the day arrives. Or the week. In the days when I worked for Ace/Charter, we had sales conferences in places like Key Biscayne or Ft. Lauderdale, San Diego, or Miami. The Ace/Charter I worked for is now out of business, having been made part of the Putnam-

Berkley/MCA publishing group. So, lately, I've been going to the Meadowlands Hilton, across the highway from Giants Stadium. There are still publishers going to Key Biscayne, and from an editorial perspective, I think there's an advantage to it; at least there is if you're one of the editors chosen to attend.

If the entire company is "away"—away from the home office, away for a period of time—it allows everyone to mingle and to talk. The talk doesn't necessarily have to be about the books being presented (though they are never far from the conversation). By getting to know each other, developing relationships between the sales reps and the editors (and anyone else attending), we are able to work more closely together. The rep is not as cautious about calling an editor for more information or seeking help with a title she's having difficulty selling. You become friends and trust each other.

There is also a difference in the meeting schedule when it is held out of town. Presentations may be made from 8:00 AM until noon; the afternoons are given over to small group meetings, to what are called "individuals," where the rep sits down with his boss, goes over all his figures, and discusses whatever needs discussing. The atmosphere is more relaxed, more congenial. (Oh, yeah, okay, it also gives me a chance to get away from the office for a few days and enjoy myself. Maybe that's why companies don't do it as often these days.)

When the conference is held in New York (and most publishers are in New York, and New Jersey is just across the street), the editors do not stay at the hotel. They go home. Which means that they have only one day and part of an evening to do everything which needs doing. The most important thing is presenting the list.

We gather in a conference room; all hotels have

them now, they need the convention and conference business. There are no windows, but there is a cloud of smoke hovering just below the ceiling. The presenters are seated behind a table stretching across the front of the room. There are some water pitchers, a couple of microphones, and a dire lack of elbow room. Someone at the table has the remote control for the projector in front of him. Behind them is a screen, making it inconvenient to look at the slide you're discussing; it's a good thing you rehearsed and know what you want to say about the changes that will be made. You do know, don't you? Oh well, it will come to mind when you get to it. If the publicity department has prepared something on videotape, there are a couple of monitors at either end of the table. Over the speaker system, the opening chords of the theme from *Rocky* pour into the room. Everything is in readiness.

You sit. Stretching into an indefinable distance are the members of the sales force and the rest of the support personnel and liaison people. If you're lucky, you're presenting first on the first day of the conference. The reps are fresh, alert, they haven't been trying to digest anything but last night's dinner. If you are presenting on the afternoon of the third day, however, when everyone is numb, when ninety other titles are swarming for space in the memory banks, well, you know you have a good presentation, so you gird yourself, take a deep breath. . . .

"Don't you think it would be better to delay publication of that book, given everything you want to do, until after late summer? After all, Warner is going to be releasing *Presumed Innocent* in May, and there just won't be any room in the stores. . . ."

As I've mentioned, editors try to keep up with the competition, try to find out as much as they can about everyone else's publishing plans, because those plans can affect their own. Here is a perfect example of what happens when we miss information or receive misinformation. The rep, being in the stores regularly, often hears about other pub dates (or other things we might be interested in knowing) before we do. We hadn't been certain about the pub date for the Turow novel, for which Warner had paid a mind-boggling $3,000,000, but expected it to be a summer release. It is the kind of book that makes great vacation reading, and we expected a June pub. The book would have shipped early in May, been on sale for the summer push. . . .

I thought I'd get around the Turow release by publishing *Trojan Gold,* the most recent Vicky Bliss mystery by Elizabeth Peters, in May, thereby establishing my place. (That we later lost the author puts the whole matter into the infamous cocked hat.) We hoped to make *Trojan Gold* the book with which we would make Peters as good a seller as she is as Barbara Michaels. We had an exciting and exotic dump display, featuring the two series characters she was famous for (Bliss and Amelia Peabody, the Victorian Egyptologist), life-size and in full color. We had changed our cover art so that it did not echo the books we had already done by this author (if you have a continuing author you try to give the covers something to make them immediately identifiable to the audience), because we were going to make this one glitzy, different, special.

Nothing we were going to do, however, would allow us to compete with the kind of push Warner was going to make on *Presumed Innocent:* Some estimates indicate they will have to sell somewhere in the neighborhood of six million copies in order to hit break-even at a $4.95 cover price.

The ironic thing is that I had originally scheduled the Peters book for July and moved it, fearing the Turow would move me right out of the line-of-sight. I just moved in the wrong direction. Fortunately, it was early on the first day and the rep was awake.

When you have a good sales force, things like that happen. Of course, the reps have a vested interest in seeing the books come out at the right time and in the right way, but far too many of them, as is the case with all people, seem to shy away from saying anything. They know that the editors have strong emotional attachments to most, if not all, of the books; they know the work we've put into getting the book to this point, and they're afraid of insulting us. Or, maybe even worse, being viewed as disputatious by their bosses. But the editors who get to go to sales conferences regularly have learned to listen to the sales force. I don't want to hear that they're going to have a problem selling something; but I want to know about it because I may be able to find the solution, either in packaging or through something the publicity department can put together; nothing is insoluble unless you don't know it needs fixing.

Reps will tell us that there's been strong resistance to a particular style of art, or that in one or another of the territories fantasy is selling but science fiction isn't. They know the books that are selling just below best seller levels, and by telling us, we may discover authors to romance away and onto our lists. They see the first indications that a new category is coming on strong, that it might be time for me to publish novels of the business world. It is the sales rep who keeps me informed as to what is going on with what bi-coastal businessmen call the fly-over people.

So I sit in that darkened room, adding the smoke of my pipe to the haze already there, and hope that they know that I am listening to them as closely as I pray they are listening to me.

And then I ad-lib. Or I did once. It was my first sales conference. I was presenting a first novel by Barry Sadler, the "Singing Sergeant," the man who had composed "The Ballad of the Green Berets." The

novel was *Casca: The Eternal Mercenary.* I thought I had
enough ammunition, given Sadler's career. Then, early
on a Sunday morning, I received the call.

"Mike?"

"Yeah."

"This is Robbie." Robbie is Barry's agent.

"Yeah."

And then Robbie proceeded to tell me that Barry
was in jail. In Nashville. Something about shooting a
man through the head, just to see the sucker dead.

Right.

When I presented the title, I casually mentioned that
Barry was available on a limited basis for publicity. I
pointed out that he would do anything to help sell the
book. I told the sales force that Barry took things very
seriously. Then, turning away as if I were finished, I
let them know that someone had annoyed Barry once
too often, and I told them what happened. Bang, bang.

The book sold.

And I learned a lesson. I've been known to draw a
pistol to emphasize a point. I've been known to use a
sword cane as a pointer. I love show biz.

By the end of the session, three or four hours after
we've begun, the reps know the company target figures
for each title we've presented. Later in the course of
the meeting, they will be given individual targets.
Often, they are asked what they can get, rather than
being told, and we adjust our figures according to that
input. These people know their customers.

And in this instance, the sales force represents the
editor's customer. You always take your customer out
for a meal or a drink, something to cement the relationship. By the time the day ends, everyone is ready
to go out and blow off some steam. I am amazed at
how much pressure builds up in that room over the
course of a few hours. And I am thankful, always,
when, over drinks, a rep will come up and say,"Oh,

about such-and-such. I think I can get . . ." For every one who speaks up, there are probably ten who feel the same way. We've sparked interest.

How do we let the rest of the world know that we're excited?

Chapter 7

WHAT DO
YOU DO HERE,
ANYWAY?

I'll be back in publicity . . .

No one seems to know who they are. We know they
hang out in back someplace, all those people, and they
have something to do with us. But what? The best way
is to say that you're going back to publicity; someone
is certain to point out that they're in promotion. Or
advertising. But not publicity.

There's a difference?

Yeah. Oh, by the way, the answer to the question
which serves as the chapter title is not "nothing," even
if it sometimes feels that way. To both you and me.

The three divisions—promotion, advertising, and publicity—are considered part of the marketing structure, and their single job—coming at it from different directions—is to *promote* the sale of the book. Even though all three *promote* your book, they're not the promotion department, but part of the marketing department.

What the promotion department worries about is the buy-in, the sale of the book to the publisher's customers. When you go to a bookstore and see a poster, the promotion department has been at work. When you receive imprinted bags or bookmarks advertising a publisher's title, someone in promotion had a hand in it. They have offered the bookseller something to make taking quantities of a particular title more attractive.

They also produce the brochures and other sales related materials. Each month, the sales reps receive kits which contain all the cover proofs for the selling month, an order form, brochures and posters (if they are applicable; posters are made infrequently because most books don't lend themselves to the approach), or mini-posters. The brochure is usually four color and four pages long. The front reproduces the cover, sometimes with additional copy, the two page spread inside is hype—whatever we can say about the book that will make it appealing and, by the act of producing the brochure, showing some of our commitment to the book. The mini-poster, or sell piece, is a single sheet, most often two color with some sales copy and an order form on the back.

Before the rep arrives at an account (and sometimes again after the sales call), these sell pieces are sent to each of the publisher's customers, either to prime the pump or reinforce the sales message. The brochures may also have details about any special displays or other items being planned.

All of these items cost money, all of them are effective to one degree or another, and they serve a single purpose—acquiring real estate.

That is the bottom line definition of what the entire process is about: getting displayed, getting display space, being seen and being seen in sufficient quantity that the reader can't help but notice you. That's one of the reasons publishers use dump displays.

It's an ugly name, dump, but if it works to get twenty-seven or thirty-six copies of your book into a store that might otherwise take only six or ten copies, you can call it whatever you want as far as I'm concerned. We'll discuss getting the dump into the store when we take a sales trip later in the process. What we're doing now is letting the bookstore know it will be available.

Just as we don't print books before the sales are made, we don't begin producing dumps beforehand either. The corrugation, the large cardboard stand which holds the display, and the tray—with nine or twelve pockets—costs out at between $2.00 and $3.00 apiece, depending on the size of the order. Because these items are generic (there's no special type on them, just the company's name), they are easy to obtain—suppliers have them in stock and run them when they're ordered. It is in the riser, or header, that the expense begins to mount. The simplest risers are all the same shape and size and the publisher has them imprinted with whatever art and message it wants. Sometimes the riser only repeats the company logo.

Then there are the special jobs. I've described the display we wanted to do for Elizabeth Peters, using life-like figures at either side, and a pyramid-shaped riser card between them for our message. That requires at least four colors, a die cutting, and hiring an artist to do the paintings. We would have had to have received orders for more than 1,200 dumps, each with thirty-six books, to make that work. What we would have had, however, is a dump we would have been able to reuse every time we released a new title by that author. Once the initial art and design work are done, and the die prepared, the expense is reduced considerably.

Because we will not have any new Elizabeth Peters titles, however (having lost her to Warner), we're going to use a dump we created for a horror display. The header on this piece is shaped like a house. The art and printing we use when we sell it for Halloween promotions make the riser look like a haunted house. With different art, and retaining the shape, we'll be able to offer something different and eye-catching for Peters, without having to create something which will only receive a one time use.

By getting the order for the dump, the bookstore is guaranteeing me display space while not having to cut his orders for my other books (because there wouldn't be room to display them all), or cutting back display space he's already committed to other publishers. The problem is that there's also limited floor space. We'll leave that one for the salesman to deal with.

Another display generator which works for both the publisher and the bookstore is the counter pack or pre-pack. Holding perhaps twelve copies of the book, the counter display fits up near the cash register—where you want your book to be; books remain an impulse item—holding them neatly and also allowing for a line or two of selling copy to be presented to the reader. Again, the drawback is one of space—will the store have room next to the cash register for your prepack?

The Mysterious Press has created one of the most striking display pieces, a solid oak table with a pocketed riser, which was offered to a limited number of specialty (mystery) bookstores. By contract, the bookstore may only display Mysterious Press publications (their books and *The Armchair Detective*) on it. Mysterious Press also supplies catalogues, book marks, and other selling aids. The one or two times I've been in stores which had the display, it was obvious that browsers had placed things there which did not belong. However, Mysterious Press, a small house, had guaranteed itself display space in each of these stores, and could count on the regular visibility of its product, both new titles and selected back list.

Would that we all could do it.

Some years ago, we did. You may remember seeing spinner racks—wire racks revolving on a narrow stand, with four or five pockets on each of three or four sides—back in the '50s or '60s. These were created by promotion departments (each had the company's name or logo in bright colors on top), as a way to do what Mysterious Press has just done and what we all do with dumps. You'll also remember that it was just as likely that you'd find a Bantam book in the Pocket Book spinner as any other. Now the spinners have gone the way of the marble-topped soda fountains they used to be placed next to. There are still some around, but fewer are being placed. Time marches on.

One of the ways we know that time is, indeed, passing, is that new books are coming out and we have to find cost-effective ways of letting the readers know. That's why a wily promotion director came up with the idea of putting the first chapter of new books at the end of current ones, a particularly effective method of promoting series novels. Another device, and one booksellers like, is to produce a pamphlet containing chapters from a number of upcoming titles. The preview booklet is a favorite approach when a publisher is promoting a new line. What better way of letting the public know that you will be releasing a horror line, and those books will be available in *this very bookstore?* The bookseller likes it because anyone picking up the pamphlet is already interested in the genre, and this will spur the customer into returning to buy the books he's just sampled.

Every once in a while, especially for books in which everyone in-house has faith but which are going to be difficult because they are first novels or the author is crossing genre, the promotion department might suggest producing advance reading copies. These are not galleys, which usually have plain printed covers and which are "uncorrected"—set from type which has not yet been proofread. Instead, a first printing of the book is done and several hundred copies are bound in a special cover. This cover might duplicate the final one, or it might have a piece of the art and some special copy, announcing that it is an advance reading copy, that it is not for sale, and—on the back cover—carry information about the things the publisher is hoping or planning to do for it. Advance reading copies for hardcover books look like trade paperbacks, while the ones made for mass market books look like, well, paperbacks.

They are a bit less expensive than the usual bound galleys because they are part of the regular print run—which means the publisher can run more copies—making them effective and sometimes impressive giveaways at the American Booksellers Association convention or as something for the sales rep to give to key accounts, those where he thinks reading the book will help get the dealer's support.

Okay, then: Promotion is point-of-purchase oriented, it is stuff, things, giveaways to the consumer or for the use of the store owner. It may make him part of the process, as with the reading copies, or remind him about the books or make it easier for him to display them—and so to sell them. In one way or another, we hope, it convinces him to buy the book, to support it, and encourages him to buy more copies than he might otherwise.

■ ■ ■

What's my ad budget ... ?

There are times when I think that book advertising is the second best ego-stroke in the world, but little more than that. For the next month or two, pick up the Sunday *Times Book Review* and compare the advertised books to the best seller list ... then draw your own conclusions. It has been my experience, anyway, that consumer advertising works best after the book has shown that it has legs, that it's already moving. A lot depends on the kind of book we're talking about. Advertising non-fiction strikes me as sensible, whereas advertising most fiction seems like wheel-spinning. Fortunately for you, I'm not in the advertising department. As your editor, I want your book mentioned everywhere, even if we have to pay for it. Paying for it is advertising.

Conventional wisdom has it that trade book publishers commit a dollar a copy for advertising, based on a projected first printing. If the orders don't come in, the advertising budget is one of the first things to go. There is no point in advertising a book which can't be found in the stores. It may be a matter of the tail wagging the dog, but there it is. That's why it is difficult to get a publisher to make the ad budget a part of the contract; those writers who get the clause don't really need the advertising. One notice that a new Ludlum novel is available is all that's necessary to make it sell out.

There are two forms of advertising—trade and consumer. Trade advertising is addressed to the book-seller, wholesaler, and library markets. The ads appear in *Publishers Weekly, Library Journal,* and the other trade magazines addressed to our customers. Coupled with a review in one of these journals, an ad can be helpful. The amount of help is undoubtedly moot since there are many publishers who do not advertise in the trades regularly and still manage to be successful. Indeed, if you pick up one of the semi-annual announcement issues of *Publishers Weekly,* you might be surprised at who hasn't taken an ad. (Maybe you won't; it could be your publisher.)

Newspaper advertising is the most familiar way of reaching the consumer, but there are other options. Magazine advertising, because of their national distribution, is prohibitively expensive, but it is possible to take an ad in the regional editions, allowing the publisher to reach a specific, targeted audience. Category publishers, in support of books which have a particular fandom, will advertise in magazines such as *Locus, Mystery Scene, The Armchair Detective,* and other publications specializing in the various genres. This form of advertising has the advantage of being relatively inexpensive and reaching exactly the market we want to address.

Working in conjunction with a good advertising agency, it is possible to buy 30-second spots on network radio. You might not be heard during drive time, but the talk stations (which are a prime candidate for advertising) have a solid, round-the-clock listener base. Alternatively, buying time on a local station (spot advertising as opposed to a network buy)—choosing it because its audience is the one you want to reach—can help bring the right book to the attention of a large, potential market.

What is particularly interesting about radio advertising is that a network buy can cost as much as a spot in a major market—$350 for a 30-second ad. (And like peanuts, one is never enough.) Added to the expense of buying time is studio rental and the cost of hiring a narrator (or two), engineers, music, and special effects. (How's this for a kick: In the time I've been writing this section I've heard ads on the radio for two different books, on two different stations. Spots, one for a paperback original, the other for a reprint by a best-selling author. Two rock stations, one crime novel, one espionage novel. Hmm.)

There have been publishers who have bought time on television to advertise titles with breakout potential, but I haven't seen a book on network TV in a long time. Some specialty publishers, such as Time-Life Books, are using the cable "superstations" to push their series, but they seem to be out there by themselves. There still are occasional television ads, but when we hear about books on TV these days, it is usually as a prize package on a game show: "Yes, Bill, you've won a selection of best-selling novels from _____, valued at over $100."

If you read the trade journals (and if you don't read *Publishers Weekly* you are making a serious mistake), you will see that the ads sometimes mention print figures and ad budgets. It has been my experience that these should be noted, but not taken as gospel.

There is another form of consumer advertising which is becoming more and more popular, and with good cause. It's called co-op, and it allows the book dealer and the publisher to work together. When a sell piece or trade ad mentions the availability of co-op money, the publisher is letting people know that it will share in the cost of advertising a particular title. The dealer is expected to take a specific number of copies, of course, and the publisher supplies the ad mat— ready-to-run art and copy for the book part of the message—and the retailer adds the name of his store, a special price if he is discounting the book, and anything else he considers pertinent. The offer of co-op money is a function of the promotion department (because it affects the buy-in), and the cost of the ad comes from the advertising department. No wonder people are confused.

■ ■ ■

The stuff that dreams are made of . . .

I'm sure you'll remember that some time ago I called and asked for a list of people you knew, the name of your local bookstore, things like that? Remember, you were going to get to it next week? Well, send it now, because we're about to go back and see those folks in publicity.

Publicity is wonderful. Publicity is, all things considered, free. Publicity can be fun. And publicity probably sells more books to the consumer than anything else you'd care to mention. (Keep it legal.) Publicity also involves you very directly, it can be done by you without any support, but if you decide to do it, suddenly you will discover that there are a lot of people behind you, ready to help. Publicity helps generate word-of-mouth, and that is more effective in getting the word out than advertising. Who are you going to believe: Your best friend or someone who is telling you exactly what they want you to hear? Right.

It is the publicity department that mails the galleys of your novel (if it is hardcover; they are rarely produced for paperbacks) to key reviewers and to anyone you suggest should get copies. Working in conjunction with your editor, they will also send them to individuals who would be willing to give you an advance quote. Using information about the book supplied by the editor in the form of the tip sheet, and by you in the form of your biography, they write the press release which will accompany not only the galleys but the review copies of the book when it's ready to go. Their goal in life is to get you noticed—and is that not the stuff of dreams?

Getting you noticed is not always easy. We can send books to reviewers, but we can't force them to review. (If we send them enough books that they ignore, we take them off the mailing list.) Working together, however, things can be made to happen.

Have you become friendly with the manager of your local bookstore, either a small shop in town or one of the chain outlets at the mall? You should. You should also let them know when the book will be available—they might be willing to sponsor a signing. (The most wonderful thing about signed books is that they can't be returned. When you're in a bookstore, offer to autograph every copy of your book you can find.) If you let your publisher know that a signing has been arranged, the publicity department will see to it that the store's order will be filled in plenty of time.

Signings can be enjoyable times. They may also be disheartening. I've sat at the side of an author—a major, bestselling name in the mystery field—at a B. Dalton's on Fifth Avenue in New York City for two hours, two hours during which only three books were bought. Another author, in Oregon, had the experience of signing only one, and then discovering that it was stolen. A lot depends on the location of the signing, the time of day, how well known you are in the area, whether or not the bookstore advertised the fact that you were going to be there, whether you are in a high visibility spot or not. But fear not, there is another side to the signing story, and I'll reveal it shortly. (That's called building suspense.)

With the proper information on hand, it may be pos-

sible to get radio or local television and newspaper interviews. The idea of getting on "The Tonight Show"
or "Today" is a very nice one, and I want you always
to keep it in mind. Just don't count on it, please. Most
of the shows on which we see authors do not take
kindly to novelists (the book has to be read, after all)
unless they are newsworthy. (Even if your book is
timely, it doesn't mean that the bookers for the big
shows are going to care. It is whether the author's
name is going to draw an audience that counts. People
will get up early to listen to Stephen King.) Local television is another matter, and if we have the weapons, we
can go on the attack.

There are also some radio programs devoted to
books—reviewing them and interviewing authors. The
publicity department sends the people producing the
shows copies of all the new books and then, if the host
expresses interest, coordinates with you. You may live
in Sheridan, Wyoming and the show may be broadcast
in Oklahoma City, but that's no problem: The telephone interview has become a way of life.

Most authors are not invited to attend the convention of the American Booksellers Association (ABA),
but if you live near the convention site, let your editor
know and he will arrange to have passes for you. If
your book is scheduled for early autumn, or if it is hot
off the presses, there may be an opportunity to set
up an autographing at the convention. The ABA is
supposed to be a selling convention—special discounts
and offers are made to the bookdealers we hope will
be attending—so having a book by you just out or coming up in the fall season is a deciding factor when the
publisher considers inviting you. Your editor, however,
if he is attending, will be more than happy to have the
opportunity to get away with you for a while, get away
from the convention floor, get away from all those
books. . . .

There are other opportunities for personal appearances, particularly if you are a category writer. There seem to be at least three science fiction conventions going on on any given weekend, mystery fans gather at the Bouchercon (at which the fan-voted Anthony Awards are presented), and the pros meet every May in New York for the Mystery Writers of America Edgar Allan Poe Award dinner. The Western Writers of America host a fun-filled, week-long celebration, culminating in the presentation of the Spur Awards, while the Science Fiction Writers of America get together to honor their talent with the Nebulas. There are fantasy conventions, romance writers conventions, gatherings for virtually every interest. And no, your publisher will not send you to them, paying your way from—where was it, Sheridan?—to wherever the convention is being held. But if you are going to be there, your editor will probably invite you to attend the dinner and will certainly spend time entertaining you. (You might be lucky and find something enjoyable to do. I know where the poker game is at Bouchercon.) The publicity department will—if they know you are going to be there—work with whoever is running the book room (a feature at most—though not all—conventions), to be sure your book is available.

It is not unheard of for writers to be invited—all expenses paid—to attend functions of this kind, but it is rare. (How can you invite one writer and not another?) You can guarantee an invitation for yourself, however: Get nominated for one of the category awards.

There are some things the publicity people can do on their own, but if you supply everything they request, either directly or through your editor, they will be able to do even more. If you take the advice of most media experts, public relations people—and other authors—you will get the ball rolling by yourself. Once it is in motion, you can call on your publisher for backup, just the way a cop does.

■ ■ ■

Bishop to king one . . .

I've already mentioned Paul Bishop's *Citadel Run.* Paul has done everything absolutely right in his efforts to support the publication of his first novel. The only thing he didn't do was legally change his name to Joseph Wambaugh. The way things are going, he may not have to.

Some background on the author. Born in England, now in his early thirties. A detective with ten years experience in the Los Angeles Police Department. Well-spoken. Active member of the mystery community, both pro and fan. Published short story writer. Now, novelist.

As soon as we bought the book, Paul said that he understood there wouldn't be much done for him. After all, this was a first novel. Would we mind if he did some things on his own? The answer was, "No, we wouldn't mind. And," he was told, "if you keep us informed, we might be able to help."

The first thing Paul did was get in touch with other police officer/writers, sending them copies of the manuscript and asking for quotes. That part was easy. (I died a thousand deaths; editors rarely consider sending manuscripts to writers. It just isn't done.)

Then he put together his own sell kit: A folder, a self-designed bookmark, an article he had done for a professional police officer's journal (about writing cops), a detailed biography, and a sketch of what he thought the cover should be. (We disagreed.) Bishop sent the kit to me and I sat down with our publicity director. Before we had started talking, he called to say that he was going to have a signing at Scene of the Crime, a specialty bookstore in Sherman Oaks. When were we publishing?

"Paul, can I finish editing the book first?"

"Sure. Call me back."

Well, it wasn't quite like that, but he was moving fast. And when we needed something, he sent it *express*. Obviously, there were other law enforcement journals. He sent us a list. We sent galleys. Another piece of advice for someone who wants to get interviewed is to supply a list of "hooks," interview topics, something with which to sell yourself. The hook was obvious—a cop writing about cops racing from Los Angeles to Las Vegas and back, during one tour of duty. (The author denies ever participating in such an event.) The L.A. papers picked up on it, and the interviews began.

In the meantime, we took on the expense of producing the kit Paul had designed, duplicating the article, adding copies of the early quotes which were coming in, as well as the material we had produced, not the least of which was the cover.

When we had a pub date, we called Paul and arranged to ship books to Scene of the Crime. I don't know what was done to promote the signing; I do know that the bookstore has an extensive mailing list. And I know that Paul signed more than two hundred copies of the book during that one afternoon.

Maybe it's just because he's Hollywood, maybe he's just a natural, but Paul didn't need media coaching—he has presence.

If you are considering pushing out, and if you have any question about your ability to deal with the media, ask your publisher to recommend a coach. Coming across badly can hurt your chances, and you don't get a second shot if you're on a local TV show. Live.

It has also been suggested that you request a video tape of any appearances you make and if you haven't had the opportunity yet, that you try to stage something and have it taped in a studio (ideally) or your home. A publicity director can use that tape to sell you to a potential interviewer. Use your hooks, those things that make you and your book special, on your videotape. (We're taking it for granted that if you have been on a talk show, the conversation dealt with you as an author.) An audio tape is not quite as effective (this is a television world, after all), but if you have one and cannot afford to produce a video, by all means send it along. As with everything else, there are no guarantees, so you might want to think twice before you make an investment.

Paul's book is getting excellent reviews and he is being favorably compared to Wambaugh and other cops-turned-writer. His publisher had nothing to do with that; it was his writing that did that, his writing which will finally "sell" the book. I knew it was a good book before it was acquired (that's why I bought it, after all) and knew that he'd be able to talk it up, and that there'd be ads in the mystery magazines because Paul is well known to their readers. I also knew that Paul was personable and would make a good interview; being able to assure the publicity manager of that helped pave the way for the department to do what it could to get the author some air time.

Paul went out of his way to set things up on his own, using his contacts, but always checking back with his contact at the publisher's office, making certain no efforts were being duplicated.

The book is moving, gaining speed, but not running away. But we're all happy, and, as this is being written, it has only been out for three weeks. We don't know where the book will finish up, how the final figures will look. But I know that when the option book arrives, and I buy it, the publicity department will be ready to go to work for Paul.

Not the least of the reasons is that he was ready—and prepared—to go to work for himself.

▪ ▪ ▪

Promotion, advertising, publicity. I don't know, finally how much each helps; I don't know how to place a value on them. I know I want to factor them into the plans for all the books I edit. I know that if I do nothing to get support from these three departments, the book will suffer. And I know that for all the jokes I make at their expense, they work very hard, under constant pressure. They may have more deadlines than any other department, more things thrown at them at the last moment—on a regular basis—than any other department. "Back in publicity" is a place of controlled frenzy, something which can't be adequately described here; it must be experienced. That's why it bothers me that you can't spend an evening with writers without hearing someone complaining about how the publisher didn't do enough in the way of promoting his book.

Funny, I've never heard them complaining about the truck driver.

Chapter 8

DOWN
THESE
MEAN
STREETS

Welcome to The Twilight Zone . . .

Almost everything your publisher has done to this point has had a single purpose: Sell your book. I really don't know how the sales reps do what they do; it makes the writing seem easy. They spend day-after-day driving from one place to another, going into stores and . . . well, you'll see.

When I joined Charter Books back in 1977, Tom Doherty encouraged me to do something I had wanted to do for a long time—go out on a sales trip. It was important, and any editor who doesn't have the opportunity (or who fails to take advantage of it) is making a serious mistake. We've prepared (or helped to prepare) all the selling tools for the reps; we've talked about the book, hyped it unashamedly, gone on at length about the story. We've given the salesperson *everything* she needs to do the job—everything except a clue as to how to present it, sell it, convince the customer to buy it, in thirty seconds or less. That's about all the time there is to present each title.

The bookseller is rarely interested in all of the who, what, when, where, why, and how of the book. He wants to know what it looks like and who wrote it (and whether or not he has sold that author). He wants to know if there are any reviews, where the book is slotted, how committed the publisher is to seeing the title or author succeed. He wants a word or two about the book and then he wants to move on. I didn't know that the first time I went out, of course, and when the rep I was traveling with suggested that I might be interested in selling my list, I jumped at the chance. It would have been nice of him to put a net out for me before I leapt.

Pete had it all down pat. Young and good-looking, he always wore white suits (I found out why, later), and if the day was gray and gloomy, he'd bring a flower for his customer, or some other little thing to brighten the moment. Unfortunately, he didn't know how to get from where he was to where he was going, which meant we were late as often as we were on time. That not only didn't endear us with the account, it made me more nervous about what I was going to do. I learned a lot from Pete—all of it wrong. I learned more and got better advice from the other reps who let me travel with them. They're not always thrilled by the prospect of having someone from the home office with them, especially someone who doesn't know what's going on. Introducing us takes time from the selling presentation, and when we see how everything we've done is reduced to a couple of sentences, the visitor tends to look askance at the salesperson.

But only once. After the first couple of minutes, one begins to understand just what is going on, what makes the difference between a good rep and a bad one. The same information is needed whether it is a wholesale, retail, or chain buyer that is being visited. (It's different when you get into the specialized educational markets.) And you begin to understand the problem. Singular. Publishing, as an industry, produces too much product. There are too many books.

■ ■ ■

So that's why they're called "Sooners" . . .

Budget is a word you'll hear a lot around a publishing house: There's the editorial budget, the amount of money an editor or editorial department has to spend on acquisitions for the year. There are the advertising, promotion, and publicity budgets. Then there's the sales budget, which is not how much they have to spend, but how much they project they will earn. Once sales has estimated what they will *earn*, it is balanced against what will be spent on promoting the sale of the book. Together, it is the marketing budget.

That marketing budget is based on what the editors have told the marketing department about the books, as well as the track record for the category generally, or the author in particular. Every house has different definitions, and trying to sort through them here would be time-consuming and counter-productive. We've talked about lead titles, the ones at the top of the list and from which we expect most in the way of orders. The second lead is a book almost as strong, but for one reason or another is approached with more caution. Mid-list is usually defined as category: These are the books which will, month-in and month-out, sell steadily, and always within the projection; there's little about them that's risky. Below-the-line books are reissues, and other books which are not expected to perform—it is a way of keeping books in print.

Most publishers release the same number of titles every month, or every season, something our customers have come to expect. Sometimes, though, a publisher will not want to take up a slot with a particular book. Certain series titles, for instance, no longer have to be presented separately each time they appear. They will become a category unto themselves. That frees a slot for a new title, allows the publisher to release one more book in that month—and increase the size of his overall list thereafter.

Super releases serve the same purpose at the other end of the spectrum. These are books with so much breakout potential that the publisher doesn't want to hurt the rest of the list by making it simply the lead title and losing sales on other titles. When a sales rep presents a book as off-list, it is a signal to the buyer that the book should be considered separately from the rest of the month's offerings.

The accounts have budgets, also. Sometimes the budget refers to the amount of space being made available to a publisher, and at other times it may refer to the amount of money allocated for the acquisition of inventory. That may be broken down in terms of total expenditures, it may refer to the amount to be spent on particular categories, or it may be money for a particular publisher.

Funny thing about budgets—people find ways of fudging them. Murphy's Law again: Another publisher will always convince the account to spend your money on his books. You want to arrive before the money's gone. You want your off-list books on the shelf.

Oklahoma got its nickname because of the land rush. The Sooners—everyone who got the good land—settled the land before the territory was officially opened. They got there sooner.

You want to get to your account sooner, too.

That's why most reps, before they left for the sales conference, will have scheduled appointments with their accounts for the first weeks after they return. Before they leave on the sell trip, they go over their notes, prepare their presentations, and gather together all the material which was mailed to them. Because of the quantities needed by each salesperson, it can't be given to them at the meeting. So, while we've presented them with one or two of everything, quantities of galleys or advance reading copies, brochures, sell pieces, gimmicks, and other promotional items are sent to their homes. Things are gathered as they are needed for each leg of the trip; the bundles placed in the trunk of the car, and another three weeks on the road begins.

It is not fun. There are some publishers who insist that lunches taken alone are not expense-accountable. (That's how I discovered Wendy's, and also how I decided that when I travel with a rep, I pick the place for lunch.)

A territory is such that every place the rep must call on is within driving distance of someplace else they have to go. While driving, the salesperson may listen to those cassette tapes we've made for them, motivational tapes, or hard rock. Whatever it is, the rep is getting primed for a land grab.

Bookstores don't grow; there is only so much room, so many racks and pockets, so many feet of shelf space. Wholesalers figure their business on the basis of the number of pockets they have in the outlets they're serving. Publishers, on the other hand, have a way of increasing the size of their lists that is entirely out of proportion with the amount of space. The situation parallels that of population density—the weaker are going to be pushed out by the stronger. The rep wants to get in and put the squeeze on, get his company's real estate and, if possible, a couple of square feet of someone else's. It bears repeating: If your book is not seen, it is not going to sell. Everything your publisher has done from the moment it acquired your book has been focused on this moment.

■ ■ ■

The Little Shop of Books ...

It may be at breakfast before the call is made, it may be in the car, may be the night before in the hotel room, but before the rep walks through the door to the bookstore, he or she has gone over a printout which has the account's records for at least the last couple of months. The figures will let the rep know what (and how much) has been bought, what's been reordered (either titles or authors), what's been returned. With that information in mind, the rep will tailor the presentation, emphasizing, for instance, the success the account has had with a particular writer or category, and pushing appropriate titles. A good rep might also skip titles in categories with which the store has had a poor sales record. The three copies the owner might have been convinced to take (and which would undoubtedly become returns, later) will be replaced by three additional copies of a "better" book.

Each rep will have a different approach to making the presentation, of course, but what the bookstore owner or manager will see are the covers, perhaps a copy of the tip sheet or a quote sheet, and that's it. The rep might mention that the author is about to begin a major talk show tour, or remind the buyer that the author is local—anything that will make the title more appealing and encourage a greater draw, or buy. If an author has a good track record in the store, the salesperson will remind the buyer of that fact—casually. Otherwise the impression is that the rep knows more about what is going on than the account does.

Sounds easy, right? Sometimes it is. But consider this: If it is a small store, one with no staff for instance, the presentation will be done sitting at the cash register. In the middle of the conversation, a customer stops in, wants to know if that book his friend was reading, the one with the blue cover and the plane on it, is available. Or, the telephone rings. The buyer has to deal with business; the rep's rhythm is broken. Both smile, shrug apologetically. The presentation resumes.

The owner might want to know if co-op advertising is available, or whether there is any advertising planned at all. He might look at a cover. He might start flipping the pages of the presentation binder on his own (something a rep will do virtually anything to prevent, because he loses control of the situation and may not be able to talk about a title because the buyer has gone right by it), then decide that he doesn't like the one *he's* turned to—the woman on the cover is too blatant, or there's too much blood, or his customers don't like books with skulls on the cover.

If the presentation is of hardcover titles, the owner might ask whether it would be possible to get one free with five, or whether the publisher is offering freight pass-through. (Books that are sold on that basis generally have the letters FPT on the front flap.) When books are sold on an FPT basis, the account receives $.50 to $.75 off his price, to cover the cost of postage.

Trade (and mass market) books are becoming very

expensive; the buyer may not feel that his customers can deal with a $19.95 cover price and that they certainly wouldn't consider it for a book "of *that* kind." (Whatever the kind is.)

If The Little Shop of Books is a specialty store, selling only science fiction or mystery titles (or children's books, religious books, occult, travel, museum—there are lots of specialty bookstores), the rep will automatically skip the titles that don't fit the profile, unless an author is crossing over; a mystery store would be interested in a science fiction title by an established suspense writer.

As the titles are shown, the rep might suggest quantities (for reasons known to no one in the world, eight copies of a lead title seems to be the rule). In many instances, the buyer will simply look at a cover, put a finger on it, and say, "three." That's it. It is only in rare instances that a book can really be "sold" to an account (just as it is impossible to "sell" an editor). The person buying the books, especially in a small bookstore, knows his customers—probably by first name. Attempting to convince him, on more than a very limited number of titles, that he really must take a particular title, works against the salesman. The rep may be successful once, but if the book performs according to the owner's prediction, as it usually will, there'll be no second chance.

If there is a display dump scheduled for the month, the buyer is shown a photographic mock-up of what it will look like and offered some incentive to take it. Because the dump will allow publishers to get another 27 or 36 books into the store—without taking up rack space, remember—they are willing to pay to get them into the stores. This payment can range from $2.00 to $4.00 for the more-or-less standard 27- or 36-copy display, and up to $12.00 that one publisher has offered for a special, three-title display, 168-copy dump.

After the front-list (or new title) presentation is made, the rep might suggest reorders on part(s) of the backlist—the books which have been on sale for some time. The suggestions are based on the information the rep studied before coming in, on a check of the shelves and racks in the store, or because an author has a new book coming out in hardcover or a current best-selling title with another house. An important consideration is the amount of time it takes for the initial order to sell out. Space is finite. If all sellouts were replaced there would soon be no room for new titles chosen from among the thousands published each month.

This is why Pete wore a white suit. At some bookstores the owner will, after the order is taken, allow the rep into the storeroom, which allows for a check of inventory and also gives the salesman an opportunity to "dress the racks." Suddenly, books which were hidden behind other books are now doing the hiding; books which were on the bottom shelf are at eye level; books with torn covers disappear to the back of the pocket, where they won't be seen. The rack looks better because the publisher's books are right *there*. Pete didn't want to dress the racks. He wanted to get into the account and out again. Sometimes he was in such a hurry, he didn't bother to stop and listen to the buyer's problems.

There are problems. Hardcover books may have arrived with damaged wrappers or the account may have been doubleshipped, or received the wrong books, and can't get anyone to authorize a return.

Books are sold fully returnable. In the case of hardcover and trade paperback titles, the publisher takes the entire book back—they can generally be used to fill back orders. For mass market titles, only the covers are returned—the books don't usually stand up to being shipped back and forth. Additionally, the mass market publisher pays freight both ways. When these costs are added to warehouse and handling charges, it becomes cost efficient to reprint and supply mint copies when movement warrants it.

There are stories that in today's economy some smaller accounts have had to pay one month's bill with the previous month's return. A dealer cannot simply return the books, however, but must receive written permission on an authorization form. Many reps will simply leave blanks with their customers, others prepare the authorization as needed. Obviously, the latter group has a better idea of what kind of business their accounts are doing.

The best sales representatives, regardless of the business, are those who pay attention to their customers' needs, and understand their problems. The small, personal bookstore provides individual service to its clientele. They can order a copy of a title because Mr. Smith-down-the-block will want to read it, and will willingly special order a title for someone. But they are facing some serious adversity. Prices and costs are going up and virtually all publishers require an account to buy a specified number of books. It is often more difficult for a small bookstore to meet the minimum than it is for the chains to do so. Volume and sophisticated selling techniques make a big difference, no matter what business you are in.

■ ■ ■

Is bigger, better . . . ?

Their average square footage is larger than that of The Little Shop of Books, and their shelves are always full. Some people complain about the selection of titles made available, but it is based on a sophisticated analysis of consumer demand. Perhaps that is why the chain bookstores, particularly B. Dalton Booksellers (now owned by Barnes & Noble) and Waldenbooks, have been accused of reducing literature to produce, of being nothing more than supermarkets. And as the supermarkets caused the closing of mom and pop grocery stores, the chains probably are responsible for driving some smaller bookshops out of business. Because they do a high volume business, and buy in great quantities, they receive better discounts than the personal bookshop does, and they can, and do, discount the books. (Neither discount affects your royalty, which is based on the list price.) They also bring books to places where they might not have been found previously (could you afford to open a bookstore in a shopping mall?), and that's a contribution that cannot be ignored. They are important, successful, and a fact of life. Most of them will special order for you; the managers are generally supportive of local writers, and their computerized systems make it possible for them to know, down to the copy, what is happening with inventory. If an author has several books that sell at a steady rate, month-after-month, the titles are placed in a special computer program which lets management know when stock drops below a certain level. The books are then automatically reordered. If a Walden or a Dalton decides to keep an eye on you, it can be very sweet, indeed.

The growth of the chains has, of course, had an enormous effect on the entire book industry. Considered key accounts because they represent such a large part of a publisher's business, they are usually called on by representatives specializing in selling to them, and often accompanied by the marketing director or the publisher. It's not quite like paying a visit to Don Corleone, but it is not too different, either. We're talking power.

When the chains are setting their budgets, the various publishing houses are invited to present lead and key titles for a particular season. These presentations are almost identical to those made at sales conferences. It is not unheard of to show up at Waldenbooks' headquarters in Connecticut, for instance, with a slide projector, sales kits, and other display material. The meeting is held in a conference room, and is attended by the buyers responsible for every category of fiction you are likely to present. This session is for highlights only and is usually for either trade or mass market, but not both. The buyers at this presentation are allocating the amount of money each publisher will receive.

If the chains decide to support a book, taking full quantities for each of their stores, a publisher may be able to increase the print run substantially. When the chains don't support a book—which could mean, at worst, passing on it completely, or, less harmfully, taking limited quantities for key stores—the book suffers. Without solid orders from the chains, the direct distribution the editor was counting on when he did the P&L falls off. Since the direct sale is so clean—33% return as opposed to the 60% projected in wholesale—having fewer copies out there really hurts. There are well over 2,000 chain outlets. Your publisher wants the support of the chains.

Any special displays, promotions, or programs that the publisher is planning are also discussed at this meeting, but no orders are taken. That's another meeting, or series of meetings: The publisher may call on the buyer for each category separately. The books are more fully discussed at these meetings than they are during a call on a bookstore, because there is more time given for the presentation.

You've been to one of the chain stores, I know. So I also know that you've seen publishers' dumps displayed there. Or you've at least seen the ones displayed up front. You may not have seen the one in back. (In fact, you may never have seen the back of the store.) Each one of those dumps may have cost the publisher up to $5.00 in a display or placement allowance. But if a publisher can get dumps into 800 stores of a chain—we're talking about 21,600 to 28,800 books—it is worth a $4,000 investment—charged against the book's promotion budget.

You may also be familiar with the Waldenbooks' clubs—they have one each for romance, mystery, and science fiction readers. If you are, you've also probably seen the newsletters they publish for members. Every blurb, announcement, review, interview, and article in those giveaways is paid for by the publisher. Whether there is any correlation between the number of copies of a title the chain might take and the publisher's support of the newsletters is, well, a matter of conjecture.

The personal touch a small, privately owned bookstore can offer is missing at the chains—just as the butcher down the block will pay more attention to the cut of meat you're receiving than will the fellow behind the counter at the A & P or Safeway. If local stores in the chain want a particular title, one that may not have been ordered by the headquarters personnel, they cannot order it directly from the publisher. The order must go through the home office . . . which makes special ordering easier, since all orders go to the same place in a single envelope. It can, however, take longer, and a chain manager may not be as motivated as an owner-manager.

It is impossible to generalize about the type of service the reader receives at a chain outlet—there are simply too many people involved. The inventory at a chain store is, of course, much greater than that which can be carried by a smaller store, and there is more room, so more backlist can be made available. The owner of The Little Shop of Books will usually know exactly what's in stock and where it can be found. A clerk at a chain may not—but it will only take the press of a computer button to let him or her know if the book is on the shelves. A press of another button will tell the manager exactly how many copies there are, how many he began the day with, and how many have been sold in any period he wants to check.

There is a story—perhaps apocryphal—told to me by the owner of a bookstore in the San Francisco area. When one of the chains was opening a branch in Berkeley, and sales reps flocked around, they were told to simply fill the racks with whatever was selling for everyone else in the area. An indication of the respect with which some representatives are considered, and of that chain's approach to bookselling. How can you beat "give the people what they want"? Far more usual, however, is the situation in which basic stock is decided by the home office and the field sales reps have virtually no influence at all.

Indeed, the chains can, at any moment, tell a publisher how a book is doing, whether the pace indicates a possible best seller, and will not only do so, but will work with the publisher to make certain the book does not go out of stock. (This isn't altruism; where one chain is found, the other isn't far away. If one is out of a book, and the other has a sufficient stock . . .)

Unquestionably, the chains have had an impact on the small bookstore, and many have been unable to compete. The impact doesn't come only from Waldenbooks and Dalton; television, video cassettes, and an increasing number of functional illiterates have taken their toll. The chain stores, beginning with more room, can also offer things a smaller store can't: Dalton has computer software outlets.

There are supermarkets—and there are greengrocers and butcher shops and vegetable stands. Most people shop at both. For the time being, at least, the same should hold true for chain bookstores and the cozy little bookshop around the corner.

Whether bigger is better is arguable; that it is worse is deniable. And in any case, chains make publishers an offer they can't refuse.

• • •

About that truck driver you didn't complain about . . .

If you'll recall the P & L we did earlier, it was projected that 75% of the mass market business was done through wholesalers (and for our considerations now, jobbers). The wholesale distribution of mass market books grew out of a well-established magazine distribution system. (The difference between a jobber and a wholesaler is that a jobber doesn't sell periodicals.) Between them, wholesalers and jobbers service more than 120,000 accounts nationwide. Both deal with hardcover books as well, but it represents a very small percentage of their business. Unlike the chains, if a wholesaler doesn't take a hardcover book, few people will ever notice. For simplicity's sake, we'll just refer to wholesalers from this point on.

Wholesalers have their racks at airports, stationery stores, train terminals—almost any place that isn't a bookstore *per se*. In fact, while some reps do manage to open new non-book markets for their companies (record stores, health food stores, etc.), the accounting processes and minimum order requirements obviate against the continued servicing of the account by a publishing company. Eventually, outlets such as these also become clients of a local wholesaler.

As real estate conscious as everyone else in the industry, a wholesaler's business is defined in running feet of shelf space and number of pockets available. While there is no formal statement of the fact, each publisher is allocated pockets based on the percentage of business that company represents for the wholesaler. A large powerhouse, such as Bantam, may have 12%, another large publisher 14%, and a smaller company 3%. The salesman's job is, once again, to try to get more of that space for his product.

On occasion, a publisher will spend what appears to be an outrageous amount of money for a book, usually in reprint. Bantam did it with *Ragtime* and *Princess Daisy;* Warner has done it with *Presumed Innocent.* There may be other business reasons for an expenditure of that nature, but most publishers agree that with a few exceptions, advances like that are designed to give the company leverage in an attempt to gain additional pockets. Because of the support an advance of that kind generates—not only in terms of promotion money, but in newspaper stories and media interest—everyone in the distribution system assumes that sales of the book to the public will be greater than might normally be expected. (It is greater, yes; it is rarely great enough to warrant that kind of money.) Therefore, all those people involved in the retailing of books immediately make room for the title; the expected demand forces the issue.

We know, however, that there is limited display space; even a dump may not give a store a sufficient number of copies. Therefore, another publisher (or publishers) loses space. A company which may have had 12 out of 100 pockets now has 15 or more. Those pockets represent increased business for the publisher; because the books are displayed and sold from those pockets, the publisher does—for some amount of time—earn the right to be there. In another month or two, when the publisher's rep makes another call, that space is there for him to use. Of course, if the books going in after these later calls do not generate the same sales, returns go up, and the publisher begins to lose the pockets one by one. It is not unheard of for the publisher to wind up with less than it started with, but that's part of a bounce effect. Like water, a publisher's display space seeks its own level.

The 60% return figure assigned to the wholesaler is a result, in part, of the always increasing number of books being published, and the publishers' attempts to get as many copies of as many titles as possible out into the marketplace. As such, it is more a symptom than the disease. One of the cures the industry has developed—a treatment for the fever, if you will—is the incentive program.

Each cover is a point of purchase ad, a small billboard promoting the book to the impulse market. Those who buy in bookstores are confirmed book buyers or they wouldn't be there. With the impulse sale in the supermarket, for instance, we may reach new readers, people who would have watched television, otherwise. If we satisfy them, we may have captured a new customer, one who may, in the end, move on to the bookstore for the larger selection it offers. Still, we do want the most effective distribution possible.

And so the cure. Each publisher has a different scheme; each scheme has the same intent: To get more copies out and have them kept out longer. The publishers pay wholesalers for achieving a certain level of sales. One of the more common plans is based on efficiency of sale and volume. Using the figures for the last three years, the publisher signs an agreement with the wholesaler indicating that the distributor will be paid a certain amount (either as a credit at the end of the year, or in cash) if orders and returns are maintained at an average level. The payment will be higher if sales go up or returns go down. This can be done on a total list basis, or can be hooked into performance matching previous experience with an author. No matter what twists and turns the program takes, the purpose is the same: Forcing the wholesaler (or bookstore; there are incentive programs for them as well) to buy high and return low.

If a publisher has a weak incentive program—because it doesn't believe in them, or because someone else has just happened to come up with a better mousetrap—it finds its returns rising throughout the year. Then, in the summer, when the wholesaler discovers that it will be impossible to make the incentive, the returns suddenly skyrocket as rack space is cleared for the publisher whose incentive money is more likely to arrive.

The various displays which have been created are made available to the wholesale market as well. They are, however, harder to sell since they must compete for space in the wholesaler's prime account, the large supermarket, with food, health and beauty aids, toys, etc. If a wholesaler does buy them, they receive a display allowance, ranging from $2.00 to $12.00 apiece. Some of the wholesale companies keep this money; most give it to the routemen, the truck drivers, the people who are responsible for setting up the display.

Finally, the truck driver.

After your editor, and maybe before, the truck driver is—if your book is in a mass market edition— the most important person in your life. Once the books have been received at the warehouse, the cartons are assorted in prepacks or loaded, as is, on trucks and the drivers begin their route. At each stop, the driver looks at the racks, decides what book to leave on display and what book to remove, puts the new titles into the pockets, and goes on. The driver has decided whether the book is at eye level or not, has decided whether or not to give a book another few days of selling time (unless it is an incentive title and has to stay out), has made a series of decisions, in fact, which dictate how well, if at all, a book will sell.

What are these decisions based upon? The same thing all decisions are based upon—several objective considerations tempered by subjectivity. It is the same throughout the industry. If a book has been on sale for four days, and only one copy has been sold, why leave it there? Maybe because the driver likes the author or the cover art. That's as good a reason as any. A better one is because one of the driver's friends, or the driver's wife, read the book and liked it. If none of those possibilities has come into play, however, those four copies come off, go out, get stripped, and come home.

It is said that best-selling western author Louis L'Amour will, whenever possible, go out early in the morning and buy coffee for the truck drivers working for the wholesaler in whatever town he happens to be visiting. And I know that when Xaviera Hollander was publicizing *The Happy Hooker,* arrangements were made for her to meet with the route men. The success of these authors, and others who've made it a habit to meet with the drivers, makes breakfast at dawn seem quite appealing.

And that's why you should complain about a truck driver and not your ad budget.

■ ■ ■

Filling in the blanks . . .

The heart of any sales call is the same. Some of the techniques may differ, not only between reps, but between types of accounts. The small bookstore owner, feeling the pressure of competition from the chains in the mall on the other side of the highway must be treated differently than the wholesaler who has just taken over the new, expanded, international airport.

All have to be treated with respect, however, not only by the rep, but by the editor as well. After all, these are the people who are making the ultimate sale. If, as an editor, I didn't listen when a rep told me something was wrong with a cover, I *have* to listen when the buyer tells me the same thing. And if I hear it from three or four buyers, I'd better do something about it. It's true that a lot of conflicting information is received as well. One wholesaler claims that reviews on covers sells books; another says keep them clean, put as little type as possible on the cover. One dealer reads the review blurbs; another doesn't bother. Flip a coin; I'll take heads.

There are some messages you take to heart: Naked women (as they would appear on an adventure novel, as opposed to the way they appear on romances) are a no-no if I want supermarket display of a title. Too much violence and gore is no good, which affects the way I'd package mysteries, men's adventure, and horror titles—if I'm concerned about getting them into supermarkets.

If a sales rep knows that a customer likes a particular type of book, or if the buyer's wife (or husband) does, an advance reading copy or set of bound galleys will be sent ahead or given directly to the person at the end of a sales visit. If a reprint from hardcover is on a mass market list, the house might buy 25 copies from the original publisher, and send them to key accounts in hopes of getting support. It is easier, after all, to sell a known quantity, and if the buyer or the buyer's spouse has read and liked something, not only is the order going to be better, but the rep's standing goes up a point or two as well.

The calls having been made, the sales materials presented, the order written, the returns authorized, the rep's job is only half done.

■ ■ ■

It's more than just taking orders . . .

Pete didn't want to get dirty, so he wore his white suit and never dressed the racks. He didn't do a lot of the follow-up that's necessary.

At the end of the day, after dinner, the salesman begins doing paperwork. The orders have to be sent to the office for processing (some companies now have the process on computer, and the rep uses a modem to send the information to order processing). Problems the customer may have encountered have to be straightened out. Things the rep has learned have to be relayed to the proper people.

Some publishers have instituted a system whereby the rep completes yet another form at the end of a sales call. The buyers' reactions to the titles presented are noted, books which may or may not be selling (regardless of the publisher) are mentioned, any trends perceived are discussed. If there has been a serious problem with a title, and the rep runs into it more than once, not only is it put on the form, it is phoned in; with enough time we might be able to correct the situation.

In one instance, a book being sold for April release was receiving no support whatsoever from the customers. At the sales conference several of the reps had expressed worry about the book. Even in the face of editorial admonitions—I kept screaming "No"—the author felt that horror was the correct category for the novel. The book had a one word title which said nothing at all—it was a character's name—and art, which was true to the book, but did nothing to capture the imagination. In presenting the book at the conference, I kept referring to the reincarnation aspects of the plot, and the attempt to gain control of the White House. There was a love story, a crime story. What there was, really, was a contemporary novel with an occult current charging through it.

The author, however, had insisted that this was a horror novel. The reps disagreed, the Publisher (the man, not the company) disagreed, but we were now committed to the process; it was too late. Time changes when the customers don't want a book.

The calls came in from all over the country—no one was taking it. We could have proceeded, printing copies to cover whatever small orders we received. It would probably have come in at 45,000 copies, a figure well below the marketing department's budget, leaving them with a deep hole to fill and leaving the editorial department with a high, unearned advance to explain when we requested more money for next year.

We cancelled the book, pulled it right out of the schedule, threw away the art (well, actually, we saved it in our stock art; we may be able to use it at some other point), threw away the cover proofs—everything that had been spent on the book up to that day was written off. I re-titled the book, making it clear that we were dealing with a reincarnation theme. We had new art created. The book was presented at the next sales conference and was upgraded on the list—as a second lead behind a super release, it has effectively become the lead for the month.

The author still isn't happy, by which I'm saddened; it is unlikely that I will receive another book. Everyone else *is* happy: The increased orders will help absorb some of the lost monies, although if we'd done it right in the first place, it would all be profit and earned royalties. As a writer, the most important thing for you to remember is that there is always someone keeping an eye on things.

That is the next part of the reps' job, and it is an absolute necessity for those members of the field force who sell to wholesalers. After the books reach the racks, the publisher's representative has to make sure the titles are being displayed (remember that truck driver), and watch for pace of sale. If a book is moving, the rep has to call the wholesale buyer—who is probably unaware of rate of sale—and point out that the book is selling and that a reorder might be in order. It is the equivalent to what was done at the end of the visit to the Little Shop of Books, but requires the salesperson to check the situation at as many as thirty or forty outlets. A big airport such as the one in Dallas/Ft. Worth or St. Louis might have that many book displays alone; it would be impossible to check them all, but a regular spot check is important and can pay big dividends: If I find out that you are selling well, I'm going to be more excited about the prospect of reading your option book.

(You are working on an option book, aren't you? You have returned the page proofs, haven't you?)

Have you been to the library, yet?

■ ■ ■

Stacks and stacks of stacks and stacks . . .

The library market for paperback books is nothing to write home about, so we won't.

Some of the larger libraries and library systems will buy directly from the publisher; most buy from a jobber such as Baker & Taylor. Such jobbers are equipped to process books for immediate shelving, *i.e.*, they provide and place the plastic outside protective wrap, glue in a pocket, add the Dewey Decimal number or another code, and provide the various cards needed for cataloguing. At this point, of course, the book becomes nonreturnable to the publisher.

The other major library supplier is a company called Brodart, which runs the McNaughton Plan. The Plan acquires titles, forwards them—processed—to those libraries which subscribe to the service, and then buys them back when they've run their course.

Sales to this market result from good reviews in magazines such as *Library Journal* (published by Bowker, the same people who bring you *Publishers Weekly*). Sales calls are made to the service companies, but category, quality, and trust are the selling tools; "selling" is beside the point. Some publishers specialize in the library market, either reprinting very old books or publishing new titles with little commercial marketing—an entire first printing might go to the libraries, with a few copies saved for mass market reprint submission.

Not every book is suitable for the school and educational markets—grades K to six—which consists of school book fairs and book clubs. (Did you belong to *Weekly Reader?*)

There's been an explosion in the school book fairs, a hopeful sign for all of us. It means children are reading again. To help get books to them, any publisher with an appropriate list will have an educational sales department, and mass market houses are not excluded.

Books are sold in case lots, with 25 to 100 copies in each case. The books are sold on a structured discount system, with a minimum order usually being 100 copies of a title. Larger book fair companies buy in print order quantities of 15,000 copies and up. Your royalty is based on the bulk sale rate in your contract. Some bring vans to the schools serviced, and the children walk through picking out what they want. Most of the other fairs bring large cases which open on hinges and become display shelves.

Some of the fairs also offer a direct mail service, supplying not only children's books, but adult titles as well.

There are three major book clubs for school children: Weekly Reader, Scholastic, and Educational Reading Service. The sales representative's goal is to get titles into the clubs' catalogues. With that accomplished, books are shipped to the warehouses in June, ready to fill orders which will begin to be placed in September.

The educational sales department might also acquire titles. If they do, it is the book clubs which are seen as the market. Not only new titles are considered; most of the classics are public domain and the market is large enough to allow more than one company to offer *Frankenstein*. Key to the educational sales are cover art and good interior illustrations (for classics) and, for a new book, adding review support from the Kliatt and Kirkus review services, *American Library Association Booklist*, and *School Library Journal*.

By now, just about anyone who might buy your book for resale has been approached (which means the reps are getting ready to start another trip). The orders— a large portion of them, anyway—have been received. Someone is getting ready to push the button; a real machine is about to go into action.

Pete was fired several weeks after I returned from my first sell trip. Between us, at three accounts in two days—in Pennsylvania, Maryland, and Washington, D.C., where we should have hit at least ten if we hadn't kept getting lost—we managed to undersell my list by 75%.

I do better, these days.

Pete manages a supermarket. The grocery kind.

Chapter 9

MEANWHILE,
BACK AT
THE RANCH

Who are all these other people . . . ?

It would be nice if everything were as orderly as the description of the process. In reality, everything is happening always. New manuscripts have arrived, new books are being considered for reprint, new problems are cropping up. And other people are getting involved, doing their jobs.

By now you will have received the uncorrected page proofs. These sheets have two pages side by side, and represent the finished text. It is your last chance to make any corrections and it is devoutly to be hoped that you are only correcting typographical, or printer's, errors. Any author or editor alteration (AA or EA) is charged for, based on the percentage of changes. Because an AA usually entails more than changing a spelling or a word—publishers are constantly receiving proofs back with entire blocks of copy moved or edited—the possibility of still more errors creeping in is very real. By the time you receive the proofs, consider them the finished book. And get them back quickly, otherwise production will be delayed.

The production department is responsible for the copy editing, for designing the page, getting the book set in type, ordering bound galleys, and trafficking all the materials necessary to get your manuscript from printout to published. They also work with the designers in planning the look of the finished page—from insertion of chapter heading art to type size.

Type size is often an important consideration, not only in terms of the legibility of the book, but in selling and pricing it. Publishers don't sell books by the pound (or by the yard, the way some interior decorators buy them), but there has to be a certain amount of bulk. (In the mass market industry, the saying used to be a penny a page in determining cover price.) When I first started buying paperbacks, you could get a Cardinal Giant for $.50 and it would be a book you would be able to spend a week reading. Those days are gone. The average cover price for a lead title is—as I write this—$3.95, and blockbusters are selling for $4.95 and even $5.95. Every year, as budgets are being prepared, publishers discuss where the line of price resistance will be drawn.

The other side of the price/size question is in how books are perceived, as products, by the accounts. A $2.95 book, which is the usual price for a category title, is not taken as seriously because it is not a "novel," nor does it have the same profit potential. Therefore, when a publisher has a book which is "bigger" than category, but only casts off at 224 pages, the first concern is finding some way to make it larger, get it up closer to 300 pages. A thicker book, with a higher price, is more appealing.

Thicker books present a special problem for mass market publishers: The thicker a book is, the fewer copies will fit in a display pocket. Where we were once able to place five to eight copies, now maybe only three or four will fit. But we want the higher number to be ordered—and displayed: Three pockets of a book catch the reader's eye. However, there are only so many pockets available. Where do you cut back? (Prices will not go down.)

At some point, though, books do get too big. Stephen King has complained that *The Stand* was edited down because production techniques and costs, at the time it was published, prohibited printing it as he wrote it. Today, with much more clout, King is having his novel reissued at full length. (Editorial discussions and critical commentary as to whether the book has to be any longer will be left for after midnight.)

Reprints from hardcover give the paperback house two options: The text can be reset—allowing the book, again—to be made longer, or the pages of the hardcover may be "shot." In that instance, the production manager negotiates with the hardcover house to use their pages. The original publisher receives a fee of about $2.50 per page, and the reprint house doesn't have to set type. As was mentioned earlier, houses which are doing both hard and soft-cover editions design the type so that it will fit in either format.

While you're going over the page proofs, the editor is going over the cover mechanicals, black and white mock-ups of the cover or wrapper, checking the spelling (can you imagine what it is like to have the mechanical come in with the author's name misspelled and spend the next month worrying about whether or not the correction was made?), and arguing with the art director or designer about all the reasons why you can't make the copy shorter. A piece of tissue paper is laid over the mechanical, with all the colors indicated. If the editor has a good color sense, seeing the words red, gold, blue, may give him some idea of what the cover will look like. If he doesn't have a color sense, an aura of foreboding surrounds everything until the proofs arrive.

At the same time, a set of proofs will be given to the editor with a note that says simply, "May I have a page one please?"

What is being asked for is the first page of a paperback book, which will appear before the title page. This is the publisher's last chance to grab the reader, and we usually use your words to do it. (Isn't that reassuring? Finally, your words are being used to sell the book to someone.) Most blurb pages are lifted from the text, a paragraph or two which the editor thought would be a grabber. If there are a lot of reviews available, there may be a couple of pages of quotes preceding the title page and the start of the book.

While it may vary from house to house, in most of them the production department assigns the ISBN— the International Standard Book Number (each publisher has a book of numbers, using them in order). The ISBNs are used for most of the industry's record keeping: orders are not made by title, but by ISBN. (If a book gets up-priced on a subsequent printing, the publisher may have to change the number for bookkeeping purposes.)

Working in conjunction with the promotion department, the production manager will also prepare the back of the book ads, those advertisements for other books on the publisher's list. Because books are bound by signature—sixteen or thirty-two pages together—there are times when having blank pages is unavoidable. Rather than waste the space, the production department keeps a file of ads, sorted by category, which can be dropped in as needed. When a title goes out of print or simply becomes dated, it is removed from the ad and the promotion manager chooses the replacement.

Your copyright is also obtained by the production department, sending copies of the finished book along with the proper forms, to Washington. The finished book!

■ ■ ■

The perfect crime . . .

Have you ever awakened early on a dull morning and decided it would be a good day to murder a paperback publishing company? Well, if the urge does hit, here's how you go about it.

Go to the office and get by the receptionist. Then, using your power to cloud men's minds, hide near the publisher's desk. Then, in a loud, deep voice announce, "We've missed the galley!" Can you spell gloom and doom? I thought you could.

Anyone within the sound of your voice will know that you are not an Admiral of the Fleet with the midnight munchies, nor are you a Roman slave waving bye-bye to your trireme. They will also know that you are not referring to a step in production. When a publisher misses the galley, it means a book hasn't shipped from the warehouse.

The manufacture and shipping of the finished mass market books is under the control of the operations manager. (Again, different companies will have different names for this person.) It is up to her to see to it that everything needed for the printing and binding of the books is at the bindery in time.

Her job begins with the setting of the print run. With the orders received—and knowing the percentage of accounts visited and whether the chain and major wholesaler figures are in—the operations manager and the director of marketing project a final sales figure for the book. With that number in mind, let us assume 75,000 copies, they check the figures on the author's previous books. If he is a clean seller with a good track record, they might order an extra 15,000 copies on the first printing. If it is a first novel, or if the author's past performance has shown few orders after the initial shipment, the overrun will be much less.

Let's look at the March releases: The decorative covers—those with embossing, foiling, or other special effects—were ordered on November 30th. The initial print order for regular covers, which take less time, was set on December 18th; the final print and bind was set during the first week of January and the galley shipped on February 1st. For April, with a shipping date of February 28th, the decorative covers were set on January 5th and the regular covers and the print and bind on January 25th. So why the panic if a galley date is missed?

The ship date represents the day that the books are being sent to the wholesalers (several days before they go to bookstores). The wholesalers are given the lead time because the books, loaded into cartons (packed 25, 50, 75, and 100 per box; the industry is standardizing, however, and soon will pack in dozens, beginning with 24 copies per carton), placed on skids, and then packed into 42-foot trailers, go first to one of about a dozen breakup points around the country. From there, they are shipped to the wholesalers' warehouses where they are unloaded, then reloaded for the route men to place on the racks. (When a retailer gets an order, the books go U.P.S. directly to the account and don't have to be reshipped. The retailer can display within hours.)

All publishers do not ship on the same day: Most of us are using the same two or three printing plants and all the books cannot be run at one time. Therefore, the books arrive at the customers' doors on a staggered basis, and that stagger is often used by a wholesaler in determining what goes out. If the dealer knows that a best seller is arriving on a certain date, he's holding pocket space for the title. If your book doesn't arrive on the 15th, when it is supposed to, and something else arrives on the 17th, that something else is going to get your real estate.

Missing the galley is usually the result of not getting the necessary materials to the printing plant on schedule. Therefore, you lose your press time. The book is run when the plant has the time to do it. (Whether the big houses have the clout to usurp the time of a smaller house is denied.) If your books come off the press late, they miss the trucks. They have to wait on the loading dock. When they arrive at the account, some other book has replaced it on the racks. There are 400+ titles processed through an average 128 pockets in the average retail outlet so all but the best-selling titles have a short shelf life (14 days at the outside and it can be as short as 5 or 7 days). Because wholesalers don't keep an extensive backlist inventory, if the delayed book arrives late enough, it could be returned without the cartons even being opened. (Everyone denies that this happens, too.) Missing the galley can effectively mean that the book disappears in that market. (You did return your page proofs, corrected properly, without a lot of resetting necessary, didn't you?)

Having shown you how to commit the perfect crime (I do specialize in suspense fiction, after all), let's deal with a crime you think you see us committing: Letting a book go out of stock. When a book goes OS or OP, it is because: 1) it has ceased to have any viable shelf life or order activity, or 2) because the operations manager blew it.

Thanks to the computer, anyone concerned with tracking figures can get information on a moment-to-moment basis. In addition to being able to call up the numbers, there is a weekly printout circulated throughout marketing, operations, and—in some houses—editorial, which serves as a hard copy reminder of what is happening. We blow it when everyone manages not to read the figures.

It gets a little strange, now. For years, mathematicians and physicists have been studying systems—the flow of weather, the flow of water or oil, the fluctuations of the commodities market, population growth; anything which, in theory, can be reduced to an equation. In the last couple of decades, it has been discovered that underlying all the orderliness of the equation, there is a literal chaos. Chaos has its own rules, but they're still being defined. (I can't make it much clearer, because I'm still trying to figure it all out. The simplistic example, used to introduce the topic, is weather. While having certain givens allows you to predict what's going to happen, you cannot be certain of what will happen at any particular spot along the track. Therefore, the flutter of a butterfly's wing on the west coast can affect what will happen in Muscatine. Sort of.)

Our systems are subject to some other form of the butterfly effect. Remember, we overprinted on the book for which we had reason to expect strong activity. With the books shipped, and the reps making their follow-up calls and visits, checking the racks and urging reorders where indicated, the operations manager watches the daily and weekly reorder figures. Years of experience has told us what to expect. A couple of weeks with a title reordering 300 or 400 copies each week; or a call from one of the chains telling us that they have sold 1,140 copies in three days, cues us. We watch the inventory figure drop. If the pace keeps up, we set a reorder. It takes approximately three to four weeks for a reprint, and 7,500 copies is about the smallest effective order a publisher can place. (For hardcovers, 1,500 copies seems to be the bottom line.)

If we expected the activity, we also ordered an extra run of covers so that they would be ready. (Ordering the covers when they are needed is both more expensive, because of the smaller quantity, and more time-consuming.) The reorder is based on the pace and whatever projection we can make about how long it will continue.

What we don't want to have happen, but which happens nonetheless, is to suddenly find ourselves with a large back order figure. Back orders are those that can't be filled because there's no stock. In the early days of a selling trip, all the books are on back order— nothing exists. If the reorders come in more heavily than expected, we have no way of filling orders. Covers have to be run, because we weren't prepared. It could take a month and a half before the books are ready to go. There's no way to guarantee that the demand will still be there. If it is, everything is fine; if it isn't, the reprinted book winds up being a return. Like the non-linear equation of the physicists, however, there's no way of knowing absolutely what to do in any particular situation. There is no answer.

An example? Okay.

In December, 1987, I published a novel, the fourth title in our series of stories about the frontier, the historical west. The first three books were a reprint from a single hardcover—because the hardcover was too long to reprint in one volume. (The retail price would have been too high and we were worried about the manufacturing quality; very large paperbacks show a marked propensity for falling apart.) This fourth title (actually the sixth book in the program) was relatively the weakest—it didn't have any of the credentials of the other five books which were by either well-known or highly promotable authors. The cover was attractive, but nothing "special."

The initial printing was 60,000 copies, which sold out immediately. Within a week, we had back orders for 4,000 copies and reprinted 7,500. The large number of back orders may have been some initial orders which arrived late, or it may have meant that a wholesaler in the Pacific Northwest, a local interest area for the book, may have had a run on it. In either event, demand was greater than we expected.

It is still possible that the 3,500 copies we have in inventory will not be enough. But there was no way in which we could support printing more than we did. We were on the horns of a dilemma—for the mid-list book, we usually wait until there is one month's inventory in stock before ordering the reprint; for a best seller, a couple of months' inventory is the rule. It is a day-by-day watch, now. (And after hours of discussion, we still don't understand why it happened with this book.)

If the operations manager had not been checking the figures, we might have discovered the situation too late to do anything about it. (In another instance, an author called me directly, telling me that he had signed 200 copies of his new hardcover at a bookstore. I let operations know that it might pay to keep an eye on the book's activity. I also tried to find out how the author got 200 people to buy a book!)

The operations manager must also be kept aware of any promotions being planned. We do an annual Halloween promotion (which was mentioned earlier), and when books likely to be included in the dump are run, extra covers are prepared early, tagging on to the original printing, then stored until we're ready to print books for the displays.

The other scenario for going OP (out of print), the lack of activity of a title, also falls into operation's sphere of influence. Because the manager knows on a daily basis what the activity is and what the inventory is, she is called in for a periodical destruction meeting. It would be nice for you, as the author, if a book could be kept in print. However, *most* titles run their course over a period of a year or so. With 400 new releases every month, there are only a few authors whose following is such that they maintain a steady rate of sale: 500 copies a month means we'll keep the author in print; 500 a year means the sale is effectively dead.

Real estate: There is only so much room in the warehouse. A small number of copies are kept available—in case we are going to reprint or for special orders—but the book is removed from the catalogue or order form.

When hardcovers reach their level, they are either remaindered or pulped. Remainders are sold to one of the companies which specialize in selling them for $2.95. They turn up in outlet catalogues or at stores like Barnes & Noble. If the inventory is too small, they are pulped (destroyed) as well. Once upon a time, orders went out through Doubleday's Operations Department: "Pulp Zelazny." Unfortunately, there was a title on press when the order went out. It was pulped as it came off the presses. That doesn't happen often. Fortunately. But the collectors love it.

Publishers do not remainder books or let them go OP easily. We are, after all, involved in a business (and hence, the mergers and takeovers). If the book is not making money, and something else is, the profitable book will be kept available in the space the other book was taking. Publishers do, however, have a term of license—the number of years during which they have the right to publish. If a book does go OP, and two years later something happens which makes a reissue viable—a new book, sudden fame, anything—the book will be reissued. They are never completely lost.

They only seem that way.

■ ■ ■

Hello, operator . . .

Our readers let us know that they can't find books, certainly the ones we may be advertising in back of the book ads. Every publisher has a reader's service which is, essentially, a mail order department. It is nice to know that the response to these ads is steady and that most of the readers seem to be ordering more than one book at a time. (The mail orders do, eventually, find their way onto the royalty printouts.)

Most publishers also have a telephone sales department. Because a sales rep can't be everywhere at once, telephone sales exist to service an account which needs books quickly and can't wait for the rep to show up again. There are also accounts which, for one reason or another, are not on anyone's route. It may be because of location or because the amount of business generated is just too small to warrant a regular call; the rep shows up once every six or seven months. The telephone sales reps, however, will call them on a monthly basis and present upcoming titles. These small accounts know about the books because of the mailings that have been going out regularly. A good phone rep can generate as much business as any other member of the sales force, and they're never late for an appointment. (And they don't have to watch the look of disbelief on the buyer's face when a presentation is made. There's something to be said for that: There's little worse than knowing your account doesn't believe you when you say that something is being supported or will work well. It can knock the legs out from under a presentation in no time at all.)

This might be a good time for a fascinating little experiment with numbers. Remember *The Lure,* the book we did a P & L on earlier, based on a 100,000 copy first printing, with all the books shipping? Now that we've gotten our orders, it might be entertaining to see how it really works out. The only other figures you'll need are those for production at various levels. Since I have the chart, I'll give you the numbers.

At 50,000 copies, the plant is $.1604, the manufacturing is $.1926. (Remember, these are per unit, so in this instance you'll be multiplying by 50,000.) At 75,000 copies we have $.1070 and $.1780. Looking at the bright side, 150,000 copies gives us $.0535 and $.1634 and a print order for 200,000 comes in at $.0401 and $.1598. Have fun. (I haven't done the math, so I don't know what's going to happen. But then, we never do.)

■ ■ ■

𝒟o we have the rights to do that ... ?

At some point, someone in the company checks the contract to see what rights the publisher has. These can range from as little as "COBE": The right to sell the book in the English language in the United States, its territories, the Philippines, and [non-] exclusively throughout the rest of the world except the British Commonwealth (excluding Canada) as constituted in 1948; to world rights, including translations, film rights—all those subsidiary rights which were negotiated when the process began. For a publisher working only in hardcover, the most important of these rights are book club and reprint. Both are sold in much the same way: The auction.

Just as you as a writer (or your agent) have to be aware of who is publishing what, and who might be a good editor for you, the subsidiary rights director has to keep a finger on the pulse of the reprint industry. (This is where the infamous publishing lunch crops up: Editors and sub-rights people meeting to go over the catalogues, see what's available, and trying to get an early look at the books in which the reprinters are interested. Like the sales rep, the editor wants to get there first, as will be explained after a couple of martinis. That's not fair; most people these days seem to be drinking Perrier or white wine spritzers. I prefer Turkey/soda/twist.)

There are fewer book clubs than there are reprinters, and many of them specialize: The Detective Book Club, for instance, or the Science Fiction Book Club. Then there are the biggies: Literary Guild and Book-of-the-Month. While the income the writer receives from a book club sale is not to be sneezed at, the most welcome result of a book club acquisition is the publicity—the book is advertised regularly by the club, keeping the title in front of the public. (I know that runs counter to my feelings about advertising; but I'm speaking as an editor, now.)

The person in the rights department, in charge of book club sales, will send galleys or manuscripts to the club editor and await a decision. Sometimes there's an outright buy; at other times the acquisition is the result of an auction. (Because the process parallels that of the reprint industry, we'll wait for the full description.)

When the publisher has foreign rights, you can count on the director of subsidiary rights going to the

Frankfurt Book Fair, the biggest international book rights fair in the world. (ABA is not supposed to be a rights fair; it is for selling, and one of the complaints the American Booksellers Association has had in recent years is that too many people are negotiating rights, not selling books.)

The Fair, held in late September or early October, has been described, by people who have attended, as being a zoo, a madhouse, and one of the circles of Hell. Appointments are made with foreign publishers and agents leaving almost no time to get from one to the other—so everyone is always running late. It is an indication of the importance of Frankfurt on the publishing calendar ... if you don't book a room by the end of October, you won't have a place to stay next year. And even if you do book a room, if you are five minutes late in arriving, you may not have a place to stay.

It is at Frankfurt that the major titles on a publisher's list are sold for foreign editions, with the Americans also buying rights for publication here. (For the children's and young adult markets, the big fair is in Bologna, Italy.) Books which aren't presented, or sold, at Frankfurt, still have a chance. Just as agents work with their counterparts in other nations, so too do the subsidiary rights directors have people representing them. The foreign agent usually receives bound galleys or finished books and then does what any agent does—starting with the most likely house, they go from door to door trying to sell the book. Your contract indicates how much you receive on these sales, and the monies show up on your royalty statement, though not necessarily in your pocket. (See clause 5B, below.)

The reprint market made the subsidiary rights director what he is today, usually a vice president of the company. There are many hardcover publishers who will not make a decision on acquisition without talking to the sub-rights people and finding out what their best guess is for income to be generated by the department. While the book, itself, should be what is considered, a good rights person can manage a sale so that a higher figure is reached.

The reprint sale is handled in a variety of ways. First, the option sale. When a reprint house buys a book by an author, the contract calls for an option for the next book by the author. (Sometimes, it will specify next book in the same genre, or featuring the same character.) The reprinter receives the new book either in manuscript or galleys, reads it—we usually have thirty days—and then calls with an offer. It may be accepted (the reprinter has probably gone up a couple of thousand dollars over the price of the last book) or, for one reason or another, rejected. There may have been a good early review, there may be interest in the author from another house, or the agent may want more because he thinks it will help the writer, get him more respect, or a greater commitment from the reprint house.

In the old days, many options contained a matching clause which meant that if the two houses could not come to terms, the book would be offered to the industry and the first reprinter could have the book by matching the highest offer received. This clause has gone the way of the dodo, to be replaced, sometimes, with a 10% topping privilege. If the offer is refused, the rights director uses the bid as a "floor," a starting point for an auction, with the floor holder having the standard 10% topping privilege. If that is agreed to, the reprinter does not participate in the auction itself, but gets a call at the end of the day and is told, "We've got 'X'; do you wish to top?" If the reprinter does, the book is his. If he doesn't, it goes to the house with the highest bid.

Auctions may also be generated without an option

situation. In one instance, a reprinter, having received an early look at something, makes an offer which the hardcover house does not believe is sufficient—for the same reasons listed above. At that time, the early bidder will leave the bid in as a floor, with a topping privilege, or may—thinking that they can come up with a "take out" bid—raise their initial offer to a level where they think no one will come to the auction. The reprinter might also decide not to floor the book, in which case the third auction situation arises, with the hardcover house creating it. Reprint editors want the early look so they can attempt to control the situation and avoid involving themselves in an auction, either by offering enough to make a deal or by obtaining the floor position.

The book will go to all reprinters (though some houses are reluctant to offer books to smaller paperback houses), with the information that the closing date is such and such. The hardcover publisher might establish its own floor, or let the book find its own level. Most hardcover houses today have either mass market or trade paperback affiliates in which they may place the book, or, as likely, they may decide that if their price isn't reached, they'll wait until the book has proven itself. This can backfire. Before we go through an auction, we'll take care of the other selling possibility.

Many publishers make a monthly mailing of all their titles to all the reprint houses. If anyone is interested in acquiring a book, the editor calls, makes his offer, and will either be given the book or, sometimes, the rights director calls around, says "I have a small offer are you interested," and then sells the book. The competing houses have to be ready to offer immediately. Usually an editor making a bid of that kind will not floor the book or stick around after the end of the day. Reprint editors will also call, on occasion, and buy a backlist title which wasn't sold previously. Again, that deal is consummated on the spot. The auction, on the other hand, can go on for days.

When a book goes up for auction, a closing notice is sent to all potential bidders. The notice will mention the floor price (and whether or not it is a house floor or a bidder's floor), topping privilege, and may also include a review package, and the hardcover house's print and sales figures (if applicable). The reprinters then begin to do P & L statements. The book is cast off so that we know how long it will be. We check to see if the book can be shot from the original hardcover rather than typeset. This would save approximately $3.00 a page in typesetting costs, but a 6 x 9 inch hardcover with small type and very full text pages, for example, can rarely be shot. Sales estimates are calculated, then a decision made.

Up until the last few years, auction bids jumped in 10% increments; that tradition seems to have fallen by the wayside today, and bids are often jumped at smaller percentages. The editors who will be bidding know how high they can go, based on the royalty figure the P & L revealed, and know when to make their move. (Do I want to get in early or wait until the end of the first round? Do I want to go for broke immediately, hoping to scare everyone away, or do I want to nickel-and-dime my way through this?) Whatever the technique decided upon, a house must bid in each round of the auction or drop out. Coming in late in the first round allows the bidder to get some feel of what's going on, the pace of the action. Getting in early guarantees getting in, though being closed out in the first round indicates that the reprinter wasn't really in the game.

The auction is conducted by phone, and the day of a big auction is one of great excitement at both ends. After the first call is made—it can come from the sub-rights director or from one of the bidders—the director begins calling each of the houses in turn, letting the contact there know that a bid of some amount has been received. The bidder either goes up, backs out, or asks if he can call back in a minute. (Some reprint editors do not have the latitude to bid on their own, even though the figures have been done beforehand. In fact, at some houses the editors do not know what the figures are. At others the editors use going-to-the-boss as a method of slowing the action.) While no one is ever told who the other bidders are, we are informed of how much the last bid was, and can usually find out how many houses are in the auction. (When an editor is participating in auctions regularly, he develops a sense about the other houses and their techniques.)

At some point—it can be by the end of the day, but I've been in auctions that went on until 9:00 PM and then continued the next day—it comes down to the high bidder and the floor holder (if there is one). Another 10% takes it.

Auctions usually do their job well and it is one of the times in business when you can be certain of honesty. Almost certain.

I was in one auction many years ago during which the rights director told me that she had a bid of $35,000. I dropped out. She didn't have the bid and because she came back to me later in the day and told me that I could have the book for my bid of $22,500, I began to wonder whether she had had any action at all. (The party no one comes to is not unheard of in this business.) As it turned out, I had been bidding against myself all day.

At another time, I had tried to buy two books from a publisher for $15,000. I was turned down, but was asked to leave the money in as a floor. I refused, my feeling being that the publisher had done nothing with or for the books, and I wasn't going to give them a starting point. Shortly after that, the books were auctioned, but there was no floor stated. My final bid was $10,000 for the two books. It was the high bid, but the rights director decided not to sell the books at that price, arguing that I had already offered $15,000. The books languished on the list for another three years. At that time I bought one of them for $3,500 and as far as I know the second has still not been reprinted.

When an auction is conducted properly, with everyone understanding the rules, it can be a lot of fun and, too, offer topics for discussion for weeks afterward. And when they go wrong, they become topics for discussion for years.

It's midnight, do you know where your book is?

Chapter 10
....
PUB DATE
AND BEYOND

What happens now . . . ?

A week or two before the galley is scheduled to ship,
labels are sent to the plant. You may not be receiving
the first books off the press, but you should have them
before they reach the stores. (With reprints the situation is different, since the contract copies are sent to
the hardcover house and they send some on to you or
your agent. That can take a while.)

The idea of a publication *date* has become something
of a joke: Books arrive when they arrive and are displayed when someone gets around to putting the books

out. The purpose of an announced date is an attempt to have some control over when reviews and press releases appear in print. (Trade reviews and stories are slated for a period of two to three months before publication. It's just something else to drive the people back in publicity mad.) Paperbacks don't even have a pub date, they have a pub month. If your friends are planning a party for you—or if you're planning one yourself—and you want to have books there, your editor should be able to give you an idea of when books will arrive. (For the signing party for *Citadel Run* which Scene of the Crime wanted to have before Christmas, the publicity department arranged to have the first copies of the book shipped express so they would be there in time.)

If there are going to be any ads, they will begin appearing some time after the publisher knows the books are in the stores. Like an athlete, it is possible to peak too soon with advertising and publicity, so you don't want to do very much before the book's generally available.

The other thing you don't want to do is rush out to buy the newspaper looking for the review. Reviewers are not timely, and a majority of books receive their notices months after pub date. Oh, yes, books the *New York Times* considers important get reviewed right away, but for the rest—even if they received advance galleys—they get around to them when they get around to them.

Reviewers are also idiosyncratic. When we published *The Amber Effect*, the first new Shell Scott mystery by Richard S. Prather in ten years, we didn't expect all the reviewers to drop everything immediately, but we did expect some attention. After all, Prather had sold over 40,000,000 copies of his books since the early '50s and he is important in the development of the private eye genre. One mystery reviewer, however, with a syndicated column—who requested an early galley—didn't review the book. So, I called and asked her why. (This is not something you want to do too often, reviewers do not like being questioned about their decisions and certainly not by people like writers and editors.) She didn't review it because it wasn't important enough. It was that simple. In Prather's case I was fortunate in that many of the fans jumped on the bandwagon and a lot of the pros were more than happy to lend their name to Prather's comeback by giving us quotes. It doesn't always work that way.

When Collins' *Spree* was published, we expected heavy review activity because Max is one of the best and the brightest of the current crop and is always well reviewed. There were about three or four published reviews. With the paperback edition scheduled, however, and no copy for the cover, I was faced with a problem. I didn't want the book to appear in paper without any "credentials," though the author's name should be credential enough. I took fifteen copies of the hardcover edition and mailed them to mystery writers across the country, asking them to read it, explaining why I wanted their comments, and even including an SASE. The mass market edition of *Spree* will not only have quotes on the front and back covers, but I now have enough material to use the quotes as a page one blurb as well.

There's one other influence on reviews appearing, and it is one I had forgotten until I began work on this section of the book. When review copies, bound books or galleys, are sent to a newspaper they are not opened by the person to whom they are addressed. Ah, there's no pretty way to put it: The books get stolen. When a new release disappears around a publisher's office, it's a pretty good sign that the book is appealing to a market. When they disappear at a newspaper, it means someone was bored. And it means the publicity director has to get another copy out to the reviewer . . . who will review the book . . . maybe . . . eventually.

We cannot do anything about the reviewers or the review media. Genre authors have an advantage—certainly those working in mass market originals do—in the fact that the fanzines pay such close attention to the categories and make certain that new titles are reviewed as quickly as possible. (Many publishers, on the other hand, do not pay much attention to the fanzines and so don't get them galleys or review material.) Your editor cannot do anything about the *New York Times* but he can see to it that local papers and special interest magazines receive the book. If you have supplied the information which was requested, and you still don't see a review, drop a note to your editor asking him to make certain copies were mailed.

And don't despair if you don't see any reviews; most books don't receive them and of those that are chosen, many are panned. Unless a bad review teaches you something about your craft, it is worthless. Most reviewers don't teach.

If you get bad reviews, read them, see if there's anything of value in them, and throw them away. It has always been my habit to mail copies of reviews to my authors, but if we get something in that's ugly or unrelievedly negative, I just keep it in my file. I might mention it and ask if the writer wants a copy, sending it if he says yes; I'm just as likely to ignore it: The editor is being reviewed along with the writer. In fact, when *Newsweek* reviewed Karleen Koen's *Through a Glass Darkly*, the notice ended with the comment that she had just received another big advance and suggested that she use the money to hire an editor. "They used to throw them in for free," the magazine said, "but publishing has changed." If I had been Koen's editor, I think I might have contemplated suicide. Or murder.

I know I would have been angry, and that anger wouldn't have done anyone any good. Which is why I tell you to throw the bad review away and forget it.

■ ■ ■

Parties, signings, and things that go bump in the night . . .

There are still occasional publication parties, but they are most often held when they're going to generate publicity, when there is something happening beyond the book. Elizabeth Taylor will get a party; most of us won't. If you live in New York, your editor might take you out to dinner; it is just as likely that he won't realize it's your pub date. Up until he had his 40th book published, the wife of a friend of mine used to throw parties celebrating the new release; now even *she* doesn't realize that it's pub date. Throw your own party, then, and if it's your first book, party until dawn; this'll never happen again.

Look at it this way: You've written a book, something each of your neighbors will insist he can do. And you've had it published, something very few—relatively—can or will ever do.

If you've been able to set up an autographing, let your publisher know. They will be able to make certain that there are enough books on hand, and may have other things available—signs or posters—which will help draw people into the store or to your table.

Some publishers have stickers, as well as other point of purchase items, which can be put on or near copies of books by local authors. If your publisher does, let your local bookstore know; many readers like to find books by their neighbors. (The sales rep may have pointed this out to the buyer, but it never hurts to remind them.)

At about this time you will also start receiving phone calls from your friends and relatives, telling you that they saw your book at Eddie's Books and Fixit Shop or that they didn't see it at the Little Shop of Books. Editors want to know when people haven't been able to find the book, but they have to have very specific information. They need to know the name of the store, the town it's in, and whether anyone asked someone in charge whether or not the book was in stock, on order, or sold out.

One of the reasons books are not in particular stores is because the retailer is on hold with the publisher. That means we're not shipping because they're not paying, or not paying quickly enough. Most retailers, when faced with a situation like that, will purchase books from a jobber or wholesaler, but the economic factor is a serious one. We also have to find out if the buyer was able to meet the minimum order requirement. The store might not carry books of the kind you wrote. But before we can do anything about getting the book into the store, we have to know which store it is. Then we can find out what is going on. Remember, the stand at the airport is not a sufficient clue.

Like a child leaving home, the book is very much on its own now. If everything we've done at the publishing house works as it is supposed to, your book is going to work as well as anyone can assure that it will. Publishing is, at best, inexact. A publisher may miss the mark, but a book is never left to sink or swim, something I hope you've come to understand from some of the examples of situations presented in the preceding pages.

And still our work is not finished.

■ ■ ■

Clause 5b, below . . .

Do I hear someone asking about royalty statements? Okay, here goes. You have been paid an advance against royalties and you're thinking back to that P & L that showed that while the writer was paid $5,000, he has earned $14,000. When is that money coming?

Royalty statements are notoriously obscure. They are supposed to tell you what you've earned, and how; they should let you know how many books were sold and what the reserve against returns is; they are supposed to give you a clear, complete picture of how your book has performed. Ninety-nine percent of the royalty statements issued by publishers in this country do not fulfill the "supposed to." They tell you a lot, but not everything.

Because it is company policy at all publishing houses not to reveal print figures, it is doubtful that you can get your editor to tell you. The reason seems to be quite simple: What was printed does not have anything to do with how many copies were distributed and sold. All too often in the past, when writers were told what was in print, they expected royalties based on that figure. Or they complained that the figure was too low, having no understanding of the process, of the fact that we printed for the orders received. It is a simple misunderstanding, but it is one which has caused enough trouble that people are now wary. Many editors feel, however, that if you want to know, it is your right to, and they'll get the figure for you. Very few of us know what the in-print figure is, though, because it doesn't mean anything to us, either, except in terms of having sufficient inventory to cover reorders.

Which brings us back to the heart of the statement: What you've earned. Most publishers' contracts stipulate that if a book hasn't been on sale for at least six months prior to the royalty date, then no statement need be issued until the end of the next royalty period. This is more easily explained: If your book was published last month, and 60,000 copies shipped at $3.95, and your royalty is 8%, your statement would reflect earnings of $18,960. However, there is no way at all to judge returns at this point; the book has just reached the marketplace. If we issued a check in the amount indicated, and then over the next six months took back 42,576 copies, your book would actually have earned only about $5,000 at that point, and returns might still be coming in. You would owe the publisher $13,000. (Yes, this is a worst case scenario.) That's why we want the book to have been on sale for a while before you get the royalty statement.

Returns are difficult to factor in, but they must be taken into consideration. Some publishers set a figure—it may be 25%, it may be 50%; it is arbitrary—and hold a reserve against returns in that amount: A percentage of either net or gross sales is deducted before the royalty is figured. Other publishing houses use a sliding scale, based on the amount of time the book has been on sale. For instance, there might be a 60% reserve for the first twelve months, 20% for the next six months, and 10% for the next six months. (The percentages are of the current *net* sales.) In neither case is the author satisfied; and in many instances, the royalty statement does not reflect what procedure the publisher is using to ascertain the reserve.

As a writer, you have several options: You might negotiate a clause in your contract which states that all reserves will be released within a certain period of time—three years seems to be average. You may, according to your contract, have the right to examine the publisher's records. This is at your expense if it is found that the publisher has not made an error. The accountant examining the books should be able to make a judgment as to whether or not the publisher is being heavy-handed. There have been horror stories about sloppy accounting procedures (you notice how I avoid using the word "chicanery"?), but under pressure from professional writers organizations, these have been virtually wiped out. The reserve against returns is, all things considered, a safety valve for both the publisher and the author and the money will, at some point, be released. (I haven't asked Don Westlake about this; it may be that here he will let me have my hamburger today and pay him on Thursday.)

During the discussion of subsidiary rights, we mentioned that the monies earned by the sale of rights will show up on your royalty statement if not in your pocket. Here's why: Under most contracts, the money earned by these sales is, first, shared with the publisher and, second, your share is applied against your advance. Here are some figures: You were paid $7,500 for the hardcover rights to your book and are sharing all subsidiary income on a 50/50 basis (which is the standard starting point). Your publisher sells the paperback rights for $5,000. Your share is $2,500, but instead of paying it to you, it is applied against your unearned advance. You now have to earn "only" $5,000 in book sales or subsidiary sales before you begin earning royalty monies. All of the subsidiary income should be reflected by your semiannual statement and if your editor has indicated that one or another of the rights has been placed, and you do not see it mentioned on the royalty statement, get in touch with him.

The editions published as a result of the subsidiary rights deals will also be earning royalties over a period of time, and those earnings, shared again with your publisher, should be showing up on your statement at some point in the future. However, pinpointing the date is difficult: A paperback reprint might not appear on the stands until two years after the negotiation, and it could be another year before your hardcover publisher receives a royalty statement from the paperback house, and then another six months before it appears on your statement.

This sharing of monies, especially the reprint income, is one of the reasons many writers like the idea of the hard/soft deal, where one house owns both rights and guarantees to publish in both formats. The income may be less (though there's no certainty about a reprint sale, anyway), but all royalties from the paperback edition belong to the writer. It is another one of those either/or situations, with the writer gambling that a sub-rights sale will be sufficiently high to make it worth sharing the money with the hardcover house. If the reprint sale isn't made, the author can always hope that the book is picked up later. Neither approach is perfect; some writers have gotten very rich because of their reprint sales.

So there it is, you've earned out, the check has come in. A small check, but still something. And you still have something else to do.

■ ■ ■

And now, for my next trick ...

At some point you should have sent something new to your editor, an outline, a completed manuscript, a letter explaining what you want to do next. Something. Anything. Depending on the point in the process which has been reached, the editor will have some idea of how things look for the future. If he was interested enough in your work in the first place, he's going to want more from you, anyway.

If you have the right kind of relationship with your editor, you've been discussing your next book for some time now. We don't usually want to see a new work immediately after concluding the deal for the "old" book; we need some time to see what's going to happen, how successful we're going to be. You, on the other hand, don't want to wait until the first book is published before you get to work on your next project. You should have some sense of how the author/editor relationship is working by the time you receive your copy of the cover proof. You've talked to the editor, you've seen his work on the manuscript, how he is packaging you, and know whether you want to continue working with him.

One of the greatest difficulties editors face when it comes to dealing with new authors is how to handle the option book. If a writer has a track record, it is easy to make a judgment and come up with the money for the next advance. When the property is unknown, there's no place to start. I have dealt with agents who understand this situation and will sell a second book for the same money received for the first and I've dealt with agents who refuse that kind of offer. If you have been able to get an agent since selling your book, let her worry about it. (If you had an agent all along, this is all beside the point anyway, but thanks for sticking with me.) If you are still alone, and at least satisfied with the way things are going, trust your editor enough to at least discuss the situation with him. Then do what *you* have to do.

The editor has one more thing to do.

■ ■ ■

The postmortem . . .

Whatever they call it, most publishers have a similar meeting. It takes place every month or so, and the books published in that month a year previously come up for discussion. Ninety percent of the returns should be in, enough that a picture of the book's history may be drawn, some decisions made, some lessons learned.

No one in this business has any idea of what makes a best seller. We guess and pontificate, point to last week's success and try to figure out what happened to this week's contender. Why did *The Name of the Rose* sell the way it did? Why did *The Hunt for Red October* become a best seller? Even the executives at Random House are shaking their heads at the appearance of *Winters' Tales* by Jonathan Winters on the *Times* Best Seller list. According to a story in the February 8, 1988 edition of *Newsweek,* they admit that their primary purpose in publishing the book was to get a chance to do Winters' autobiography. Why do other writers, ones with consistently excellent reviews, never break out?

There are no answers; no definitive ones, at any rate. As with most things, we can learn more from our mistakes than our successes. At the postmortem, we look at the books, at the cover proofs (because sometimes they're different and the change was made during or after the sell trip), recall the reviews and other attention the book received, and try to figure out why things happened the way they did. We've made some discoveries through this process, learned something about the way the wholesale and retail markets perceive fantasy, for instance, and how it should be presented to them. We've learned something about blood on covers and how it should be handled. We've made a discovery about the use of flags and of political symbols like the swastika and the hammer and sickle. The lessons are applied the next time.

Publishing is subject to fads. One year so-called Yuppie fiction is big, the next year it will be something else. We've watched the rise and fall of the gothic, the rise and fall of the romance. We've seen movie and television tie-ins become so popular that publishers were hiring scouts to work Hollywood, and we've seen the scouts disappear along with the books they were bringing us.

There is one constant in all of this, and it remains even in the face of trends which are dominating the field at any given moment—a good storyteller always finds a market. It may not make him a wealthy man with one book (God does smile, but not always), but the skills, talents, and abilities, the craft you've learned and what you've learned to do with it, will always be in demand. Mainstream publishers provide a service, and there will always be a publisher willing to put you through the process because you entertain us all. That is the business we're in.

Together.

Chapter 11

=====================================

NEGOTIATING
YOUR BOOK
CONTRACT

It is the best of times; it is the worst of times. The manuscript you mailed off into the void has been accepted. An editor calls. Sweet-voiced and excited, she makes an offer: So much in advance, so much in royalties. Little else is said. You respond, "Yes, yes." The contract is in the mail, you are told. If you have any questions, feel free to call, you are told.

The contract arrives. You have questions. You are also nervous: If you start making waves now, will the manuscript arrive by return mail? Will you alienate this kind editor, creating a negative force around the publication of your book? Just what *can* you do, how far can you push? Have you made a serious mistake in agreeing to the offer you received over the phone?

Having an agent, of course, relieves you of the pressure; but we know how difficult it is to find an agent these days. Forewarned, however, being forearmed, and knowing that editors usually have some room to negotiate—and are willing to do so—you are no longer alone.

I've taken several standard contracts, amalgamated them, played with them, and here offer you a look at the typical book contract, at your options, and where and how hard you can push to protect yourself. Having an agent is still better, but with this information you will be able to speak intelligently and knowledgeably to the editor who calls. Thus being more comfortable, you will be able to negotiate the best possible contract for yourself.

Contracts begin simply enough: The Publisher is named, the Author is named (and perhaps a pseudonym, if you have chosen to use one). Then the contract begins:

THE PARTIES AGREE AS FOLLOWS:

■ ■ ■

1. Grant of Rights

The grant of rights is what the Publisher is acquiring, and it lists everything you are selling. It generally begins with the words *The Author hereby grants and assigns exclusively to the Publisher and its successors, representatives and assigns the rights in and to an unpublished work of fiction [or nonfiction] tentatively entitled:*

That "tentatively entitled" is sacrosanct. You may think that your title is brilliant; as with so much in publishing, however, the marketing department may have some very different ideas. For instance, certain words are thought to have a negative impact on buyers, and publishers want to avoid them. The editor may know of another book with the same title that has just been released (it happened to me recently; fortunately my novel is still in outline). Whatever the reasons, good editors will work with you to select a title. This is also the last time the title of the book appears in the contract; hereinafter it is called the "Work." The Publisher acquires rights for the full term of copyright and all renewals and extensions thereof

> in all languages throughout the World, includ-
> ing all US military installations, the right to
> print, publish and/or license and sell the Work,
> in a hardcover and/or paperback edition or any
> part or abridgment thereof. And the rights of
> digest, condensation, anthology, quotation,
> book club, first serialization, second serializa-
> tion, TV and performance rights, with exclusive
> authority to dispose of such rights.

That's the *boilerplate,* the wording that's part of the printed contract before changes are made. The Publisher has acquired *all rights to your work* in every form imaginable. (Some contracts also mention "or forms yet to be devised or developed," which takes care of whatever may come along tomorrow.)

An agent would begin by striking out the translation rights, world rights, performance rights and, as often as not, first serialization rights. Your agent is in a position to sell those rights for you, and it thus makes sense for him to retain them. The Publisher also has representatives attempting to place rights throughout the world. If your Publisher places the rights, you'll receive a percentage of the monies earned, usually 50%. If your agent places them, you receive 100% of the monies, less the agent's commission. (And, in both instances, the representatives in foreign countries or in Hollywood also take a percentage, which is deducted from the top.) The problem you face, *right now*, is that you don't have an agent and it is virtually impossible for you to place most of those rights yourself—you don't have the contacts. The editor you're dealing with knows this and will make a good case for being allowed to retain the rights. You, however, are thinking of getting an agent now that you have a track record . . . but you can't count on it. What to do?

Ask the editor to amend the clause so that the rights in question revert to you if the Publisher hasn't placed them within 18 months of publication. This allows the Publisher to try to do that part of the job (which it will—selling such rights represents additional income, after all), and still protects you. If the Publisher hasn't sold the rights, and you have now acquired representation, your agent will be able to go to bat for you.

In agented acquisitions, the rights sold are usually for publication in the United States, its territories, the Philippines and Canada, and are for English-language publication only. The Publisher generally receives book club, second serialization, anthology, condensation and abridgment rights, as well. (It is also standard for the Publisher to retain the right to allow Braille or other editions for use by the physically handicapped to be produced at no fee and with no royalty.)

The next clause is generally the copyright clause, which authorizes the Publisher to copyright the work in your name and guarantees that the copyright notice will appear according to US Copyright Law and the Universal Copyright Convention. You agree to protect the copyright, and that if you dispose of any rights you've retained, you will see to it that the proper notice appears. There's nothing here for you to worry about.

■ ■ ■

2. Delivery of Manuscript

You've sold a completed manuscript. At least, that's what you thought. But changes may be requested. (Or you may have gotten lucky beyond all expectations and sold your book from an outline.) The first lines of this clause read:

> The Author agrees to deliver to the Publisher a manuscript of _____ words on or before _____. Such manuscript shall be a complete and legible copy of the Work, properly prepared for the press and in form and content acceptable to the Publisher.

So far, it's easy. You know how to do a word count to prepare a manuscript. But "form and content acceptable to the Publisher"?

That's where the editing comes in. If the editor thinks the book isn't ready for press, the Publisher can demand changes:

> Publisher shall notify Author within _____ days of its receipt of the manuscript as to its acceptability or nonacceptability. If, in the sole opinion of the Publisher, the Work is unacceptable to the Publisher, the Publisher shall provide the Author with a detailed list of reasonably required changes, and the Author shall have _____ days from the receipt of said list to make changes. If, in the sole opinion of the Publisher, the revised Work is unacceptable to the Publisher, the Publisher may reject it by written notice within _____ days of delivery of the revised manuscript, and may thereby cancel this Agreement.

Upon such cancellation, the Author will repay
to the Publisher all sums of money advanced.

You have the right to expect your editor to work with
you. In the wording in this delivery clause, the editor
is required to tell you exactly what is wrong and to
make specific suggestions as to how to correct the problems. (You're right if you're thinking that that's pretty
much the definition of an editor. Unfortunately, not
all editors live up to the definition.)

The sticking point might be the words *sole opinion of
the Publisher*. Most publishers won't change that and
trying to get it changed is undoubtedly an exercise in
futility; certainly, there's no way to get two immovable
forces to move. You might try, however, to amend the
words *Upon such cancellation . . . money advanced* so that
you have a *first proceeds* right. Simply, such wording
permits you to repay the advance if and when you
resell the manuscript in question.

This is a time for good faith, on the part of both
parties. If you're selling your first book, odds are the
editor has already discussed the changes she wants with
you, and you know whether you a) agree and b) accept
the suggestions. If you don't agree and accept, or if
you feel that you can't do the work requested, you
won't have reached this stage of negotiation. A good
editor will also recognize your intent and integrity as
a storyteller, and shouldn't be asking for things that
change the point of your work.

It is certainly easier for an established author to get
a first proceeds clause; publishers have every reason to
believe that the author will be in a position to repay
because he or she will be in a more realistic position
to resell. (And, too, the author may have an ongoing
relationship with the editor or publisher. An author
recently sent me a book that was not only unacceptable,
but also—for him—unfixable. Because of our relation-

ship, we were able to agree on the delivery of a different book entirely ... one he was more comfortable with and one I knew he could do without encountering problems.) You may have to be a judge of human character in deciding how far to push here, deciding whether you "trust" the editor with whom you are dealing. If you don't, you shouldn't have gone this far.

The amount of time to allow for the work called for (all those blanks in the quoted paragraph) is probably negotiable. It's not unreasonable to expect reactions within 60 days; by the same token, the Publisher should be able to count on you to do the necessary work in the same amount of time. The rest of the delivery clause will often refer to rights, permissions and non-text items. If you're quoting from someone else's work, if you're using a line from a popular song, if there are maps or other supplementary matter, it's your responsibility to acquire all the rights and permissions to use those items ... in *every* territory licensed to the Publisher. Those rights are often expensive, and you are solely responsible for the expenses.

In the contract we are using, you have sold hardcover and paperback rights (a situation that pertains more and more often these days). The person selling you the rights to the quote or the song or the map will ask about the number of editions, territories, etc., and will charge accordingly. (Permission to use lyrics often comes at a price that will make you seriously reconsider whether your character should sing a song, or simply hum it.)

▪ ▪ ▪

3. Editing of Manuscript

After you've done your rewriting, the editor and copy editor begin work. According to your contract:

> The Publisher has the right, in its discretion, to make any editorial changes in the Work deemed necessary by it, with the Author's approval, which shall not be unreasonably withheld. The Publisher also has the right to request additional material or revision of the Work from the Author. The Publisher will make the final decision on title, cover art, format, and retail price of the Work. In the event the Author is more than one person, the Publisher shall determine the order of authorship credits.

You have the right (in fact, it may be demanded of you) to see the edited and/or copy-edited manuscript, to check it, and to discuss any problems with your editor. Editors rarely work by *caveat,* and the changes in your manuscript have been made to ensure better reviews and better sales, and to prevent embarrassment to either Publisher or Author. Editors have enough to do day-to-day to guarantee they won't make changes capriciously.

We've discussed the title; don't bother arguing about cover art or format (hardcover, trade paperback, paperback). These are tied to marketing decisions that represent the Publisher's informed opinion as to how to best sell the book. There are certain authors who, by dint of their position in the firmament, may be able to approve covers, but they are few and far between. If your book is in a special category, or it in some way reflects specialized knowledge (e.g., a historical book set in a period which you know backward and forward) you might suggest that you supply stock art—examples of period clothing, perhaps—and offer to look at the sketches for the cover art to be certain that a character is not depicted carrying a weapon that hasn't yet been invented. (Do you get the idea that this may have happened to me?) However, it will be virtually impossible for you to change the wording in this clause, and you are well advised to trust in your editor. Again, everything is being done to help the sale, not hurt it.

If you've done your homework and research, it's safe to assume that you're already familiar with the kinds of cover packages your Publisher uses. If you've laughed every time you've seen a particular publisher's packaging, you wouldn't have submitted to that publisher. So don't worry about it.

■ ■ ■

4. Copy-Edited Manuscript and Page Proofs

Most contracts give you the right (and *obligation*) to read, correct and approve your Work in both of these production stages. If the contract you receive doesn't, demand it. You'll be given from ten to twenty days (depending on the Publisher's production schedules) to do this work. You want to catch editing problems— changes that somehow negatively affect your work— now, because you will be charged for changes you make in the page proofs. Make certain the clause states clearly that you're not responsible for "printer's errors in accurately reproducing the approved copy-edited manuscript."

If that clause isn't in your contract, you may be surprised by what appears in the finished book. If you don't do your checking quickly and accurately, you have no one to blame but yourself. If your Publisher refuses to agree to a clause giving you the right to approve the manuscript and page proofs, find out why.

• • •

5. *Warranty and Indemnity*

This clause will appear in every contract. It is something no editor will change, no attorney will allow to be deleted. There are, however, some things you might wish to discuss, depending on the nature of the book.

> The Author warrants and represents that he or she is the sole proprietor of said Work and has full power to make this Agreement and grants that it in no way infringes upon the copyright or proprietary right of others and that it is original and not in the public domain and that it contains no libelous matter and does not invade the right of privacy of anyone. The Author agrees to indemnify and hold harmless the Publisher and Seller of the Work against loss or expense, including court costs and reasonable attorney's fees, incurred by it by reason of any finally sustained claim that said Work violates any rights whatsoever. All warranties and indemnification hereunder shall survive the termination of this Agreement.

You are guaranteeing that you have the right to sell the Work and that it contains no libelous material. Given the readiness of people to sue these days, it's reasonable to expect that your Publisher wants to be protected. This clause doesn't give you something you might want—the right to agree to any out-of-court settlement—but it does specify that any action must be "finally sustained." If it's a nuisance suit, then you aren't responsible for any costs; if the suit is valid, well, you blew it.

Also watch out for a warranty clause that mentions obscenity. No one has a definition of obscenity worth the paper it's printed on right now, and you may have used a dirty word or two. Most editors are aware of the general community standards and will protect you in the editing, but whether you want to *warrant* that the Work is not obscene is a matter of personal choice.

Keep in mind, though, that no editor has the authority to make any changes in this clause, and that it is rarely, if ever, changed in any way.

■ ■ ■

6. Advance

When your editor called, she told you she'd pay a certain amount for the rights to your book. *Then* was the time to decide whether you would accept the offer. Don't accept, wait for the contract to arrive, then ask for more . . . it's too late. If you're unsure and want to talk to friends, do it before you say yes to the deal. Just tell the editor, during your initial discussion, that you "want to think about it" and will get back to her. Indeed, if you aren't satisfied with the offer, those words should represent your manuscript. Don't feel pushed or pressured. Don't let your emotions rule you. Don't say that you're checking with your best friend, your spouse, or an agent you met five years ago. As in writing, the principle is Keep It Simple, Stupid.

I should point out that while an editor may have

some room to maneuver at this point, advances are not arbitrarily decided. Many factors go into arriving at the figure (not the least of which is the boss saying, *"That's what you're going to offer!"*). Editors work with profit-and-loss worksheets, forms that take into account sales in the category, production costs, cover costs, royalties, freight costs ... the list goes on. After a certain amount of grunting and groaning over a calculator, a figure is arrived at, and the offer made. The astronomical advances you read about in the papers are newsworthy only because they are so far from the norm. Whether you want to accept $3,000 or hold out for more is up to you. Don't forget, however, that the advance is *against royalties* (that is, the advance is a portion of royalties paid upfront, but which must be recouped by the publisher before further royalties will be paid); if the book has legs and outsells everyone's reasonable expectations, you will be making more money in the future.

Generally, the advance clause reads:

> The Publisher agrees to pay the Author as an advance against all earnings hereunder the sum of _____ payable as follows:

Note first, that the advance is not only against royalties but also against "all earnings." That takes into account all the subsidiary rights you've signed over to the Publisher. Every penny of your earnings is accounted against the advance, helping you "earn out."

What follows the words *payable as follows*? It's likely that the editor didn't mention the "split" on the phone, and you didn't think to ask—it wasn't something you were expecting.

The most common split is 50:50, with half the advance money coming to you on signing, the other half on delivery of the *finally accepted* manuscript: You may also run across signing and publication splits, which give the Publisher another 18-24 months to hold onto your money. If money doesn't mean that much to you (did I really say that?), you may be willing to accept that second split; odds are that the editor will, after some hemming and hawing, agree to an acceptance payment, especially if the advance is $7,500 or lower.

As the amount of the advance goes up, payout becomes more creative. On a $50,000 hard/soft contract, for instance (you are receiving that amount; the Publisher will do a hardcover edition followed in a year or so by a paperback edition), you may be offered $20,000 on signing, $15,000 on delivery, and $15,000 on publication of the hardcover edition.

The variations on the theme are endless; authors who receive multimillion-dollar contracts aren't receiving the money in one lump sum; few writers receive advance money all at once. It is not unheard of, when the amount is small, for an author to receive the full advance on signing. In those instances, the editor knows that the book is complete and that the writer could use the extra grand right away, and the Publisher is willing to agree as a sign of both good faith and good will. Keep in mind that the editor does not necessarily have the authority to agree on her own and might very well do the same thing you're doing: Tell you that she'll have to get back to you . . . even if she already knows whether or not she's going to agree. That's what makes it fun, right?

The standard split, however, is half on signing, half on acceptance. You can ask for something different if you are offered anything else (especially at the lower end of the advance spectrum). Make certain, though, that you agree on the split before the contract is drawn up.

■ ■ ■

7. Royalties

Hardcover royalties are standard in the industry: 10% on the first 5,000 copies, 12½% on the next 5,000, and 15% thereafter. Your editor will simply say "standard" or "10, 12½, 15." If she does say standard, check to make certain her standard is the same as yours.

Paperback royalties are all over the board. Certainly, you should try to get a 6% royalty as the minimum. A royalty offer of 2% or 4% is not unheard of.

It's possible to negotiate the point: you might ask for a split, the most common coming when 150,000 copies are sold. If you begin at 6%, the royalty jumps to 8. If you begin at 8 (more usual if you are established), the jump goes to 10. If you begin at 10, take the offer and run.

Royalties, like advances, are not arbitrary; they are factored into the profit-and-loss sheet the editor prepared, and are considered, rightly, an expense by the Publisher. Keep in mind that while you're receiving your percentage based on the full cover price (at least you should—your contract should specify "retail" instead of "net" price), the Publisher is selling the book at a discount—perhaps as much as 50% off. Ideally, the estimated royalty payment will be equal to, or more than, the advance. Not so ideally, you have no idea of what the sales are going to be (and the editor has but a little more information), so it's difficult for you to find the balance point.

You can, for your own pleasure, do some simple math that might give you a ballpark figure. For instance, in the case of a hardcover book, estimate—for a first novel in a popular category—that you won't sell more than 4,000 copies. Multiply by an average cover price of, say, $14.95. That brings you to $59,800. Now, multiply by 10%: $5,980 is what might be expected as earned royalties; therefore, an advance of between $5,000 and 6,000 is reasonable. *Please* keep in mind that this is a very rough way of estimating, that it takes none of the other expenses of publishing a book into account, and is—at best—an informed guess as to what the book will earn in royalties based on a rough guess of sales. While the same paperwork may be done in order to ascertain mass-market royalties, it is impossible to offer estimated sales figures for you to use in your computations; the market is simply too volatile and a sales estimate may as easily be 35,000 copies as 135,000.

The rest of the royalties clause lists other types of sales: These are special sales, remainders, premiums, sales for export through mail-order, etc. The Publisher earns less on these sales than on normal ones; therefore your royalty will be lower. You will be told that no royalty will be paid on review copies, damaged copies, or those sold below manufacturing cost. I've yet to hear of a successful negotiation on most of those subparagraphs, and the reason, I think, is no one bothers. The lower royalties exist because of exchange rates, bulk discounts and other such factors. Given everything else you must think about, I think you can just make sure nothing seems outrageous in the contract you receive, and if you are bothered, ask the editor for an explanation.

Another subclause in this section will make it clear that "copies" refers only to copies in a particular format, and that the specific royalty breakdowns apply only to specific formats. In other words, you can't lump your paperback sales together with your hardcover sales, and expect hardcover royalties on the total. Eminently fair.

■ ■ ■

8. Subsidiary Rights

When you granted your Publisher all those rights in paragraph 1, you weren't giving them up for free. In most cases, you will receive a 50:50 split of subsidiary rights sales. Here it's important to understand the principle of "flow-through" in order to know exactly what you're getting.

Here's an example: Your Publisher has sold rights to a French publisher for an edition in that language, and received $3,000. Half of that is yours, half is your Publisher's. *However,* your half "flows through," becoming the "earnings hereunder" we looked at under point #6. If you haven't yet earned out your advance, your money is applied against the advance. (There are contracts that still call for unearned portions of the advance to be repaid. I can't recollect that clause ever being invoked; but you don't want it there anyway.)

It is only after the book has, through royalties and other sales, earned back the advance that your percentage goes into your pocket as cash. Your royalty statement should list every bit of this income, however, whether or not it is still flowing through. If your editor tells you of a sale, and your next statement doesn't reflect it, call. It's possible that the monies didn't arrive until after the statement closing date; it's also possible that someone made a mistake.

Some writers have attempted to insert into the contract a subclause stating that once the book has earned out, any monies received from subsidiary sales shall be paid immediately to the Author. The more usual procedure is for that money to be accounted for at royalty time and, as you can imagine, changing that procedure is difficult. It means setting up a separate accounting procedure and even in this day of computers and data bases, publishers are reluctant to do this. You might consider using it as a bargaining chip: Request it and then give in—in exchange for something more important to you. '

It's also possible to change the percentages. You might be able to request, and receive, a 75:25 or even 90:10 split on movie rights, for instance, and most editors are amenable to that change. Remember, the usual split *is* 50:50, and on most of the so-called standard rights (paperback reprint, book club, second serial) there's little room to maneuver.

Make certain that all the rights being sold, and the percentages being paid, are spelled out clearly, and check back to the first page, where the grant of rights appears first, to make certain that nothing has been left out: Because both the subrights paragraph and the grant paragraph are part of the boilerplate, it's always possible for a correction made in one to be missed in the other.

You have the right, at the time the offer is tendered, to ask just what rights are being acquired and it's wiser to make changes then, rather than waiting for the completed contract to be in your hands.

■ ■ ■

9. Reports and Payments

This paragraph in the contract explains the Publisher's fiscal cycle: when the accounting procedure comes to an end, and when the royalty report will be drawn up. Each publisher uses different timing, based on its own fiscal calendar, and you're not going to change it.

There will also be a clause that states that the first statement won't be issued unless it covers a period of more than six months from the date of the Work's first publication. That means that if your book is released in the last month of an accounting period, you must wait until the next period for a statement. The reasoning is simple: In the first month the Publisher has absolutely no idea of how the book is doing and what the "returns" are going to be. Bookstores may order, say, 5,000 copies of your book. But that doesn't mean you have sold 5,000 copies, as the stores have the right to return unsold copies. Therefore, the Publisher will report the number of bookstore orders, minus an anticipated number of books that will eventually be returned. This is called the reserve against returns. Because the Publisher has no way of estimating a reserve against returns, a statement prepared too soon after the book goes on sale could earn you a payment that far exceeds the book's real earnings.

Some contracts call for the return of overpayment, either in cash or by applying the amount against future earnings; others make no mention of the problem.

You can understand why a publisher would want to protect itself in cases like this, and it is, therefore, a clause that is virtually untouchable. Some contracts specify the reserve against returns, others never mention it. In all cases, though, publishers take it. The rule of thumb is that returns are in (or at least 90% of them are) after a year on sale.

You can attempt to pin the Publisher down, requesting that the reserve figure be made part of the contract. (The lower the reserve figure, the better for you.) Most editors do not have the right to grant it and most publishers refuse to even discuss the matter. Professional organizations, such as the Science Fiction Writers of America, are lobbying to change this situation and at some point in the future we may see it not only get into the contract but also appear on the royalty statement. There's no way of telling how long it will take, nor how successful the writers will be.

If you're going to attempt to have the reserve written in, don't push the matter and if the editor offers a

50% reserve, accept it, especially in mass market where the returns—as I write—are averaging well over 65%, industrywide. Another approach is to request a clause that calls for the release of the reserve after four royalty periods.

A reasonably standard subclause in this section of the contract states that if the royalty figure is below a specified amount (between $25 and $50, usually), the Publisher isn't obligated to pay the amount or issue a statement, and may defer it until the next period. You can usually amend that to read that you will receive the statement and you can fight for the money, too. Publishers don't think it is worth fighting over, but it's also the kind of argument that can leave a bad taste in the editor's mouth.

You also should have the right to examine the Publisher's books and records. The boilerplate on this clause (in those contracts in which it appears) grants you the right to have your representative, during regular business hours, come to the Publisher's office and examine the books . . . not more often than once a year. You are required to bear the expense of such examination, unless it is discovered that the errors come to more than a specified percentage (usually 10%) of the total sum to your disadvantage. In other words, if you've been jobbed, the Publisher not only pays you, but also pays for the discovery.

Any royalty statements you receive are binding, unless you let the Publisher know, in writing and specifically, of any objections. The letter should be received within a year of the date of the statement. Cashing a check generally signifies your agreement to the amount.

■ ■ ■

10. Free Copies

Your contract should offer you some copies of your finished book, and allow you to acquire additional copies at a discount. Ten seems to be the usual number of free copies; you can request more. Check for any language indicating the manner in which you will pay for additional books: Can you have them charged against your royalty account, or must you pay? Some publishers hesitate to allow authors to bill against royalties, because it's possible that the book won't earn any. (Sorry about that.) Your commitment here is to not sell the books you're receiving; they are intended for your personal use. While some contracts will have language pertaining to that, others don't. Rest assured, however, that if you suddenly order 5,000 copies of your book, someone is going to notice.

■ ■ ■

11. Reversion of Rights

The Publisher has acquired rights for term of copyright; this doesn't mean, though, that you've lost control for that period of time. The contract should have a reversion clause:

> If, after _____ years from publication the Work is out of print, and the Publisher, on receipt of a certified letter from the Author requesting that the Work be reprinted, either refuses to reprint the Work or within—— months of said receipt has failed to do so, or commence work on a new edition, then the license herein granted shall automatically terminate, and all rights herein granted shall revert

to the Author, except that any sublicensing arrangement granted pursuant to this Agreement will continue in full force and effect.

The number of years varies—anywhere from five to seven seems to be the boilerplate special; you'll never get anyone to agree to less than five, and they may push for nine. You don't have to give in; compromise works.

The final phrase in the above clause also prohibits you from getting full rights to license arrangements back. If your Publisher has sold rights in England and the book is still selling there, you will continue to share in that income until such time as the sublicense expires.

The Publisher will have the right to sell off any copies printed and in stock prior to the date of notification. And, while it may not be in the contract you receive, you should ask that a sentence be added giving you the right to acquire, at cost, any copies that will be remaindered (that is, sold off to discount marketers) at this time. (Actually, a clause to this effect may appear in the royalty section. In any event, you want the right to acquire overstock, at cost, before the book is remaindered.)

If the book is being reverted, make certain your Publisher is obligated to let you know of any licensing agreements in force. This not only lets you know the state of your business at that time, but also prevents a less-than-scrupulous publisher from making a quick deal (to sell off some rights that should belong to you). This becomes especially important in those instances where a reversion clause disallows a reversion if any licensing agreements are in effect. Wherever possible, you would prefer wording similar to that in the example.

■ ■ ■

12. Mandated Publication

You have the right to have your book appear within a reasonable amount of time. What's reasonable? A year is too short—most schedules are done well in advance of that kind of thing. Eighteen to twenty-four months seems reasonable to me; any longer than that is outrageous. The clock should start ticking when the manuscript is accepted; you've done all that's been asked of you; now it is up to the Publisher to perform.

Additionally, if the wording does not appear, try for something like this:

> In the event the Publisher shall fail to publish and distribute the Work by said date, then upon receipt of a certified letter from the Author demanding that the Publisher do so, if the Publisher either refuses to publish or arrange publication, or within _____ months has failed to do so, then this Agreement shall terminate and all rights hereunder shall revert to the Author, and the Author shall retain any payments made under this agreement.

This gives you everything, including the money. The Publisher may want to add (if it isn't already in the contract) an "Acts of God" sentence, allowing more time to publish in the event that floods, famine, war, and other things—such as strikes—that are out of the Publisher's control are the reason for delay. The extra time is equal to the amount of time the Act of God has been interfering.

● ● ●

13. Option

The option clause may very well be one of the most difficult and controversial in a publishing contract. To some writers it represents an attempt by the Publisher to hold an author in unwilling servitude. From the Publisher's point of view, it's there for your protection, a sign of commitment on the part of the Publisher, a guarantee that the Publisher will support the book you've signed to do, and ensure that the investment it's making won't be lost, that the book won't be a one-shot.

The essential boilerplate of the option clause is pretty much the same from contract to contract, publisher to publisher. It is in the differences, however, that many problems lie.

> The Publisher shall be offered the Author's next work in this genre at least forty-five (45) days before another publisher. Should the Publisher offer to publish that book and should the Author thereupon refuse the terms offered by the Publisher, the Author may offer to another publisher but not contract without first notifying Publisher of terms and offering Publisher the opportunity to match that offer.

The first thing to note are the words *next work in this genre*. This means the Author is free to write something else and place it with a different publisher, without showing it to the option holder. Whether you would want to do that is something you will want to consider and undoubtedly will want to discuss with your editor. If you are, however, planning to move back and forth between historical romances and hard-boiled detection, make certain the option clause has built-in limitations. This can be in the form used in

175
■■■■■■

our example, or stated as "the next work in this series," "next work with the same characters," or "next work of this kind." (That last choice leaves the door open for some nasty debate, obviously.) What you definitely don't want is a clause that calls for the submission of "the next work," without any limitation or discussion of what that might be.

The next key phrase is the one referring to the amount of time the Publisher has in which to tender an offer for rights. In our example, you must receive an answer within 45 days. Others range between 30 and 90 days. To me, 45-60 days seems reasonable, from both sides of the desk.

The last two lines of the example also allow for some negotiation. We've quoted what is called a *matching option*, because it permits the Publisher to match any other offer you receive, and acquire the book for that amount. (The "amount" may also include hardcover guarantees, royalty rates, and other terms of the offer.) As always, there are variations on the theme, and you have to decide what you want, and then see what you can get.

The most common variant is the *topping clause*: In most instances, that allows the Publisher to acquire the rights by bettering your best other offer by 10%. It might be possible to keep the option to a simple "first look." In those cases, the Publisher has a given amount of time in which to respond to your new manuscript; if you don't accept the offer made at that time, and are unable to reach a compromise, your obligation to the Publisher is complete. Because you aren't committed to negotiating, however, this is an approach that publishers are not eager to accept.

Looking back at our sample clause, you'll notice there are some things not mentioned. For instance, there's no indication of how much material must be submitted to fulfill the intent of the clause. Are you free to simply send an outline, or must you send an entire manuscript? Most agents will probably fight for an outline (and, perhaps, allow for a couple of chapters); your editor, however, may not be comfortable with that at this point in your career. To a great degree, the editor's decision may be based on how comfortable she is with you and your work, and how well you take direction—and at this point in your relationship most of these factors are unknowns.

Another item that doesn't appear above—and that I mention because it does appear in some contracts—also involves timing. The contract in which I saw this clause gives the Publisher 90 days to respond. So far, so good. The kicker is that the clock doesn't begin to run until 90 days after the publication of the last book on a two-book contract.

The Author who signed this particular contract was facing a no-win decision, compounded by some other nasty clauses. The original contract gave the Publisher rights in perpetuity to his pseudonym, an option on the next work in the genre, and an unbearably long time in which to make a decision. The two books originally contracted for had been delivered; the pub schedule, however, had book #2 not being released for two more years. By contract, then, the Author was effectively blocked from doing any further work under the name he had developed—a name that had begun to have a following in the marketplace.

There are two simple lessons in that unfortunate tale: First, unless you have contracted to write an episode in a series under an already established house name, *never* give a publisher the rights to a pen name . . . unless you have no intention of using it again.

Second, the Publisher must agree to deal with the option book in a reasonable amount of time. There are understandable reasons a publisher might not want to consider an option title before the first book is released (and why you might not want to have it considered yet. Are all, if there's no track record, there's nothing available to your editor on which to base an increased advance, right?).

Options are part of every contract and no editor will strike the clause, though I can't imagine why a writer would suggest it. In the final analysis, editors don't want disgruntled writers, and if things are not going well, the option won't be exercised.

■ ■ ■

14. Laws, Etc

Most contracts contain a bankruptcy clause that will— in the event the economy takes a downturn and the Publisher does, too—give you back all the rights in your work. If it isn't there, you want it; otherwise, the Publisher may try to sell your contract as an asset.

It has happened more often than any of us like.

There will also be notification that the laws of a particular state will govern the contract, that any changes must be made in writing, and that the Publisher's obligations under the contract may not be assigned. After 25 years, I've come to the point where I don't even look at that clause.

There are some other things you may want to look for and/or request: Try to get an advertising clause, which prevents the Publisher from placing any advertising in your book, except for its other books. Once upon a time, as the story begins, publishers sold space in their books to cigarette manufacturers and others. The writer didn't share in the income thus derived. Book club ads and the Publisher's own mail-order card help all writers; it's obvious that your book will be advertised in someone else's. Most ad clauses limit the Publisher to advertising its own product.

Look out for the contract that gives the Publisher exclusive rights to your name (or pen name), characters, situations, etc. Some houses do this and if you agree to it, the Publisher can hire someone else to write books under your name and with your characters. Publishers do this in case a writer decides to stop working on the series; after investing in the creation, publishers want to protect their position.

Finally, if you're signing a multiple-book contract, which may be offered if the editor sees the opportunity to develop a series (or if she just wants to tie you up for a while because of blazing talent), keep it to no more than three books at a time, and make certain the option clause calls for negotiation rather than subsequent titles being sold under the same terms as the original contract. Make certain that you have the opportunity to take the series and characters elsewhere if the option negotiations fall apart. Selling a series to a new publisher is not always easy (they want to know why the original house is no longer doing the books), but you want to keep your options open.

MICHAEL SEIDMAN, a thirty-year veteran of the publishing industry, is the Mystery Editor at Walker and Company. In 1987 he was the recipient of the first American Mystery Award as Best Book Editor, and was a nominee for the Award as Best Horror Editor in 1991. From 1980 to 1989, he was also the Editor of *The Armchair Detective*, the Edgar Award-winning journal of comment, review, and criticism of criminous fiction.

Mr. Seidman is a correspondent for *Writer's Digest* magazine and a columnist for *Mystery Scene*. His short story, "The Dream That Follows Darkness," was a nominee for the Spur Award, presented by the Western Writers of America, in 1988.

In addition to his editing and writing chores, Mr. Seidman is a popular guest speaker at conferences and workshops where he lectures on publishing and writing matters.

He is presently at work on a new book about writing and publishing, scheduled for release in the Spring, 1993.